"BOOTS TO BRIEFCASES"

JACK BORDEN COUNTRY LAWYER
Toils – Trials - Tales

Jack and Edith Borden

Shawna Gentry, Jack, Stacy Baker
(Editor-Is this the real reason Jack keeps coming to his office at age 94?)

"BOOTS TO BRIEFCASES"
JACK BORDEN COUNTRY LAWYER
Toils – Trials - Tales

Including the early life of the Borden Family and Jack's education from first grade through his college days. Then his days as District Attorney in the Parker County Courthouse and also when he was Mayor of Weatherford and over 60 years as a practicing attorney in Parker County. Plus his early day memories of the Courthouse Square and some of the people he remembers. His travels all over the world are mentioned as are good times of the past.

Proceeds from this book will benefit:
Abandoned Cemetery Assn. of Parker Co.
Meals on Wheels
K.P. Home
Weatherford College Scholarship Fund

This book is the second in a series of historical books Spotlighting Weatherford and Parker County planned by:

Nebo Valley Press
Leon Tanner and Mary Kemp
260l S. Main St.
Weatherford, Texas

Leon Tanner   Mary Kemp

BN 0-9726133-1-5

The Book Makers

ACKNOWLEDGEMENTS WITH THANKS TO ALL

Court Reporter, Sharon Mims; Weatherford Democrat employees: Ann Pinson, Heather Reifsnyder, and Sarah Slee: Mr. PageMaker himself - Nick Detherage and Les and Cecilia Lopez, photo specialist. Those who came running when Mary's computer decided to rest and had to be brought back to life were Kaleb Kemp, Judd White, Zane Kemp, Debbie and Rusty Kemp. And to the many friends who so gracioulsy answered my questions over the telephone-you all helped make this book.

TO THE TEXAS BUTANE COMPANY, *Judy, Janie, and all, we say "Thank You" for marketing all books for Nebo Valley Press and the ACA. Without you we feel sure we would be standing on the street corners waving out books in the air.*

NAME CONTEST COMMITTEE: *Many thanks to Jean Bryan, Herbert Fowler, Carolyn Glenn, Dr. Don Huff and Ann Saunders for giving of their time to judge the Name Contest and help select a suitable name for the Jack Borden book. Without you, it was such a difficult decision, we might have called it just "BOOK".*

AND THE WINNERS WERE: RANDI WHEELER AND WANDA TODD. *Of course both are Parker County residents and you will find their actual name entries at the back of the book and you will see how we combined these two entiries to come up with one.*

TO MY ENTIRE FAMILY: *Thanks for being so understanding when I could not baby-sit, dog-sit, assist with busy offices at the Wagon Yard and Texas Butane Co. or patch blue jeans. During this "Book Compiling Time" I have been blessed with my 6th great granddaughter and before the book goes on sale, my 7th great granddaughter will be born. Who could want more?*

AND TO LEON TANNER-*Get the plans for the next book ready. Thanks for plannning; pushing and encouraging me or this one would never have been finished. MARY KEMP*

CONTENTS

Foreword

A COUNTRY LAWYER

Before this book was titled, I ask Jack what the name of the book would be. His eyes sparkled and he had a sheepish grin on his face, and he said "Well, I guess they could call it a Country Lawyer."

Jack Borden is a Country Lawyer; one who personifies the old adage "You can take the boy out of the country, but you can never take the country out of the boy.'

Jack left the country some eighty years ago, but fortunately for us, over those years he never lost that genuine sense of country values that you "tell it like it is, or like it was, or even like it will be."

Its reminiscent of the days when people expected you to tell the truth, unvarnished, come what may! That's particularly the way it was in the country when Jack was growing up, and it shaped his life from then until now.

As you read this book, you can't help but be amazed at Jacks incredible memory and recollection of events and circumstances, and more importantly, of people who were a part of his life story for nearly ninety-five years. People who contributed to the values he lives by and shares with us in this book are real.

As he tells the stories, some funny, some happy, some sad, but in them all, that same element of truth stands out and we have no doubt that's the way it was. Like it or not!

Jack's early life in the country was not particularly an easy life. His family, like most rural families, were just getting by. Perhaps it was those early years on the farm, difficult years, that fired his determination to do something different, to rise above it. He was going to be a lawyer, go to college, law school, practice law. Pretty heady stuff for the son of a tenant farmer, a share cropper. But he did just that and through it all, his hopes and dreams were realized, and he became a lawyer, A COUNTRY LAWYER. And as they say, the rest is history.

Jacks love of the law, and life, and people is so meaningfully reflected in his stories. It makes you wonder what influenced him the most? What made him so sensitive to the needs and emotions of all these people he tells about? What gave him the uncanny ability to relate to people of every kind, the rich, the poor, the good, the bad?

Whatever it was, we can only be thankful that he has shared with us in the pages that follow, the true story of his amazing life and those many experiences that made him what he always wanted to be, A COUNTRY LAWYER.

Jack Borden was my first law partner, my mentor and will always be my friend.

Roy J. Grogan, Sr.

Introduction

"BOOTS TO BRIEFCASES"

Compiled by Leon Tanner and Mary Kemp

IN THE BEGINNING – Or as we started compiling this book- Leon and I were sure this would be a good book. About the second interview, we realized this would be a great book. Later we said : "This is going to be a fabulous book," Now at the finish of the Jack Borden story, we can only say "It is all of the above and a one of a kind book.

As we consider the life of Jack Borden and his wife, Edith Jordan Borden, we have come to realize that there will never be another story such as this. But if we, and Jack, had the time, another book could be written with all new subject matter. There is no end to the tales of Jack Borden that he has accumulated in the past ninety-four years. As has been said before, he wears many hats. He will long be remembered as Son, Husband, Brother, Uncle, Cowboy, Farmer, Student, Deacon, Pythian, Mason, Neighbor, Counselor, A Dad Burn Lawyer and a very special name: POPCORN JACK. Leon and I will never forget our special and interesting interviews with Jack, where we talked to much and caused him to wander off the subject . But that is how we picked up some of the wonderful stories. And I might add that we had to delete some names and words to make this the great book it is.

I, like Jack, was raised as a sharecroppers daughter. Although he was born on the east side of Parker County in Borden Valley and I was born on the south side of Parker County in Nebo Valley, many miles and years apart, we certainly shared many of the same aspects of country life. I am sure at the time we were growing up, neither of us realized how rough it was on our parents during the Great Depression. Fact is, most of our neighbors were in the same sort of circumstances so it was just a way of life. This book has caused me to look back on my early life with respect to all, and I am sure it will do the same for those who read it.

It has been a privilege and honor to be a part of this great adventure in Parker County History with Jack Borden. I think I speak for Leon Tanner, as well as myself in saying "Thank You" to not only Jack, but to all who have assisted us in getting this book to print.

Mary Kemp

JACK BORDEN

EARLY YEARS

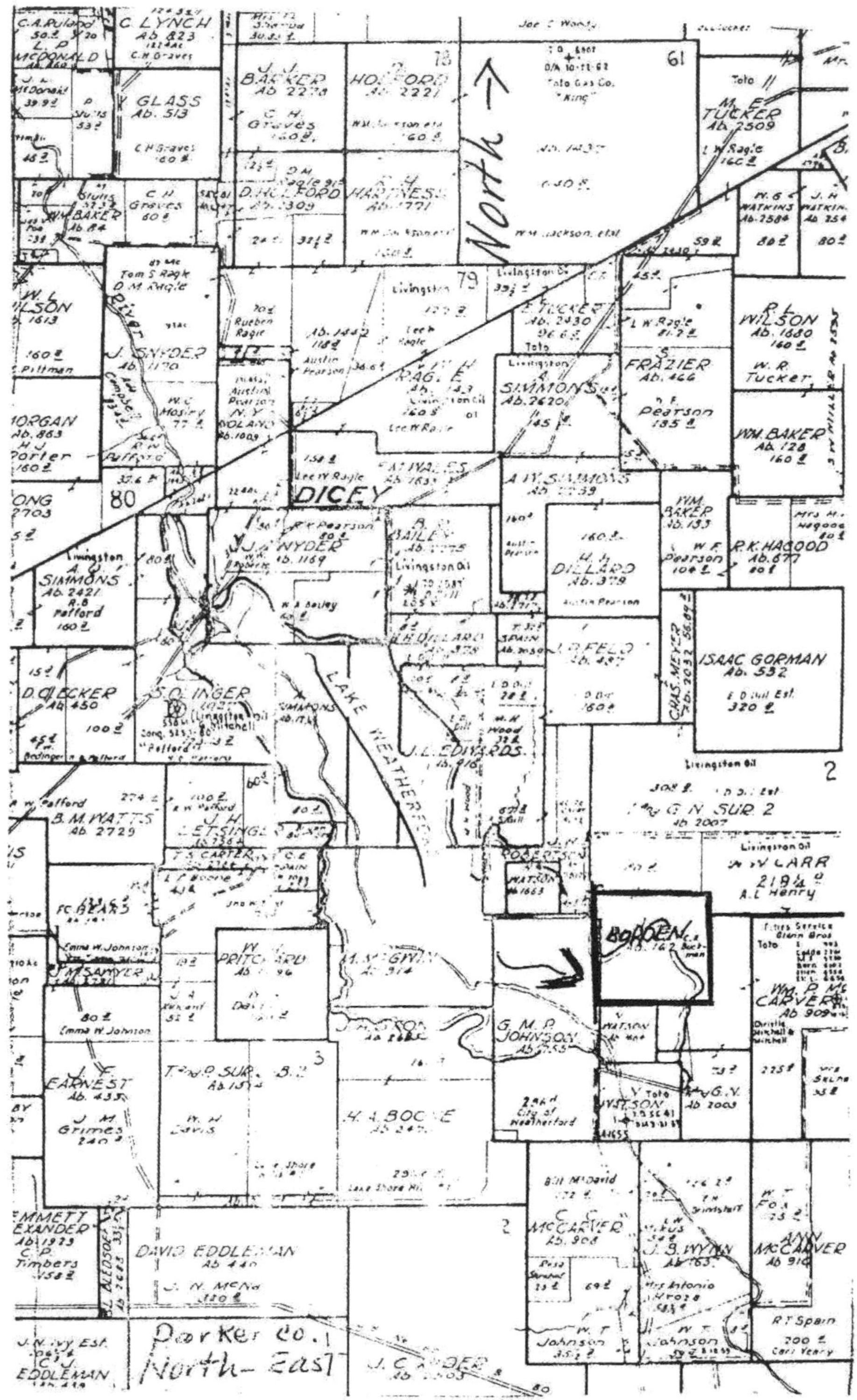
C. LYNCH
Ab. 823
GLASS
Ab. 513
J. J. BARKER
HOLFORD
Ab. 2221
North →
Toto Gas Co.
M. E. TUCKER
Ab. 2509
D. HOLFORD
WM. BAKER
W. L. WILSON
Ab. 1613
J. SNYDER
River
MORGAN
Ab. 863
Porter
Livingston
Tom S. Ragle
E. TUCKER
Ab. 2430
R. L. WILSON
Ab. 1680
S. FRAZIER
Ab. 466
Pearson
W. H. RAGLE
SIMMONS
WM. BAKER
Ab. 128
DICEY
80
79
61
A. W. SIMMONS
WM. BAKER
R. K. HAGOOD
Ab. 677
J. A. SNYDER
Ab. 1169
B. M. BAILEY
Livingston Oil
Ab. 2421
H. DILLARD
Ab. 379
ISAAC GORMAN
Ab. 532
CHAS. MEYER
D. CLECKER
Ab. 450
S. OLINGER
LAKE WEATHERFORD
J. L. EDWARDS
Livingston Oil
2
B. M. WATTS
Ab. 2729
T. S. CARTER
G. N. SUR. 2
Ab. 2007
W. V. CARR
A. L. Henry
FC BEARS
BORDEN
M. SAWYER
Emma W. Johnson
W. PRITCHARD
M. MCGWIN
WM. P. MCCARVER
Ab. 909
G. M. P. JOHNSON
J. F. EARNEST
Ab. 433
J. M. Grimes
3
H. A. BOONE
City of Weatherford
Lake Shore Hills
2
C. C. McCARVER
J. B. WYNN
ANN McCARVER
Ab. 910
DAVID EDDLEMAN
Ab. 440
J. N. McNa
EMMETT
C. P. Timbers
Parker Co.
North-East
J. C. RYDER
EDDLEMAN
W. T. Johnson
R. T. Spain
80

Farm, Family, and Borden-Dicey Schools

Jack Borden-In his "young" days

Jack Borden was born August 5, 1908, eight miles East of Weatherford on Clear Fork Creek, now a part of Lake Weatherford. Lake Weatherford covers most of the original Borden Lands, the place of Jack's birth on land patented by the State of Texas to his grandfather, Major Alexander Borden (1841-1885), and about 300 feet from where his father, John Samuel Borden (1883-1955) was born. Jack's mothers name was Bess Wallis (1885-1975) who came from Georgia to Aledo at the age of 8 years. Her parents and some relatives were sponsored by Mr. Overmire of Aledo. Jack was the third of six children: Willie Mae, Finis Cleveland (who died in infancy in 1907), Jack, C. B., Erma Neal and Sammye. C.B., Sammye and Jack are the ones still living. Erma Neal was the mother of Jacks Law Partner and Nephew, John Westoff.

Jack states: " I grew up in what was then known as the Borden Community. We were what was known as Tenant Farmers or Share Croppers, meaning the owner received a share of the crops and the tenant the balance. Tenants who financed themselves, that is furnished all labor, equipment, etc., as we did, the owner received one-third of wheat and oats and one-fourth of row crops like cotton and corn. The reason for the difference was a lot more labor was used in growing row crops. My grandmother Borden owned the 320 acres we farmed."

"During the Indian Raids in Parker County, a Malitia was formed for the purpose of defending against the Indians and chasing them back across the Red River. My Grandfather Borden was a member of the Malitia. As a result of his service my Grandmother Borden received a pension from the Federal Government. To my knowledge she was the only person in Parker County to receive such a pension. W.H. Hutcheson, a local attorney, assisted my Grandmother in obtaining this pension in the early 1920's."

Jack further states: "My early schooling was at Borden School. I think its real name was Mt. Pleasant. I once had a Certificate of Perfect Attendance for one year at Mt. Pleasant School District signed by Virgil Shadle, the County School Superintendent. Later he was Vice-President of Merchants and Farmers State Bank, Weatherford, Texas. I suppose the reason for calling it Borden was that my grandmother gave the land to the school district. In the beginning it was a two teacher school and first thru twelve grade classes. Everyone walked to school. The King children and the Vick children walked across our place to school. One of the Vick boys was Gabe Vick's father and another Vick was Winnie Chastain's father."

Jack "says" he was a model student both in attendance and deportment. The reason? The teachers roomed and boarded with the Bordens, and Jack's father told him when he started to school that if he got a whipping at school, he'd get another when he got home. Knowing what his Dad's whippings were like, made it easy to be a model student, especially since the teacher lived with them. One of the teachers was Della Crosslin, who was Ray Crosslin's Aunt.

Jack's schooling began at Borden School where he finished the 8th grade and then he went to Dicey School where they taught through high school. C. B. was three grades behind Jack, but he transferred to Dicey at the same time.

A great story as only Jack could tell: " Oh, goodness gracious, as kids, you know, you'd get into all kind of things. We didn't have automobiles in those days, but we rode a horse when we started to Dicey school. We rode a horse that three miles to school and there were other kids in the neighborhood that rode horses. I remember "Ole Preacher Wood", who lived about halfway between us and the school and he had a little horse named Trixie. Ours was named Shorty, and Trixie and Shorty were about the same size. You know boys, we'd get to racing on the way home from school. And, you'd hear those telephones click and those old blinds would go up. When we got home, Mama would say, "Okay, you boys have been racing those horses. You're going to get a whipping." And we did.

Whippings: The simple word "Whipping" means a lot to Jack and us older people. This story goes: "Not long ago my brother "C.B." and I were talking about the old days. C.B said: "You know, Mother was sort of mean." Jack said: "What are you talking about?" C. B. said: "You know when we'd do something wrong, she'd say, 'Okay, you boys are going to get a whipping.' But she wouldn't do it then. She'd wait two or three days and say, 'Okay, Boys, go cut me a switch." Here we'd been worried about it two or three days and knowing we're going to get it but didn't know when it was coming. Now Dad was different. If you did something wrong, whatever was handy, he picked it up and that's what we got whipped with.

It might be bridle reins or whatever – never a baseball bat or ax handle or anything like that."

Another good story about Dicey School and Preacher Wood. Now a lot of people thought "Preacher" was Norman Wood's real name. But it wasn't. Here's how he came to be called "Preacher". When he was in the fourth or fifth grade at Dicey he had a part in a little play. The teacher got him to learn how to recite the alphabet backwards and forward. When his time came, he started with Z and went to A. Then he turned around and came back the other way, and he'd go in the middle and every once in a while he'd just bear down on something. From then on he was known as "Preacher". A lot of people never knew his real name "Norman".

C.B. Borden, Sam Borden, and Jack Borden

DICEY'S BOYS AND GIRLS BASKETBALL TEAM

1925 Dicey Basketball Team- Benny Bailey, Joe Bailey Marsh, Charlie Miller, Jack Borden, Preacher Wood, Lloyd Hall, Coach Schindler

Dicey Girls Basketball Team -1923- Ruth Hutcheson, Teacher standing. Faye Mabry Beavers, Vivian McDonald Schindler, Josie Hall Ragle, Ruby Sharpe Wilson, Olive Marsh, and Bessie Ragle Gilbert.

"At the country schools during my time, the only sport we engaged in was basketball. The basketball courts were outside and the court was dirt. It was pretty rough. Needless to say, almost all of the boys tried to play basketball. There were a half dozen of us that had been trying to play basketball since we were large enough. At Dicey we had what we thought was a pretty good basketball team. At the end of the season, Dicey and Whitt were the only two undefeated basketball teams in ourt category in the County."

We thought we were pretty good. In fact we beat Whitt, us boys, in 1925 for the County Championship. We played up at the old Central High School, later Weatherford Junior High School, where the City Hall is today. Now Miss Vera Priddy taught at Dicey and her brother Mac Priddy was at Whitt. Miss Vera told all the parents at Dicey to be loud and supportive and she would handle her brother. She stood right beside Mac Priddy and everytime he tried to intervene or help Whitt, Miss Vera would step on his toes real hard. Jack says: "We won." Later, Miss Vera married a Mr. Ragle.

In the Fall of 1925 Jack was transferred to Weatherford High School to finish his education. He drove from the farm and back daily in a Model T Ford. You would think the next paragraph would tell about Jack's high school graduation – but that comes later.

*Old Central High School
Weatherford, Texas*

LEAVING THE FARM

Jack says "We did pretty well on the farm until after World War I. About 1917 or 1918 thru 1925 farming for us was not good. Two or three times when we had a poor crop year we did not have enough money to put in the next year's crop. We would move to town and Dad would get a job and with the exception of the horses and cattle the land was idle. After a year, Dad had saved enough money to try again and we would move back to the farm. 1925 was a disastrous year so Dad decided to call it quits."

A number of dad's friends, also farmers in Parker County, had moved to Yuma, Arizona. Among them was George Newman, a former neighbor. His son Pete later was Sheriff of Yuma County. Dad decided to go to Yuma. The plans were that Dad and C.B. would leave January l, 1926. My mother, and my sisters and I were to come when I graduated from high school in the spring. Early January l, 1926, when Dad and C.B. got in the car I got in also. Dad said "What do you think you are doing?" I told him I was going to Yuma. After a lengthy argument he said O.K , get your clothes, and I said they are already in the car. So, I became a high school dropout.

It took us seven days to drive a model T Ford from Weatherford to Yuma, AZ. We were received with open arms by all of the Parker County farmers. Since none of us knew anything other than farm work, all three started working on farms. There was a Chinese grocery store close to where we lived. One day Dad was at the grocery store and Ling Su, the owner, said, "Mr. Borden, me no understand, me Chinese me come over here, stay 8 or 10 years, no speak good English. You Texan come out here and stay 6 months and you speak pretty good English."

In about a year my dad, my brother and I decided that farming was not for us. I got a job at a hardware store as delivery boy. Not long after I began work there, they began selling electric refrigerators, a brand new thing to me. They employed a young man from Los Angeles to do the repair work. Yuma life was not for him, so he quit. The company sent me to Los Angeles to an electric refrigeration school, and I became the refrigeration expert. My parents later moved to Hemet, CA where there was a bunch of good Parker County people. Dad owned and operated what is now called a Convenience Store. In early 1929, mother, dad and the younger girls returned to Weatherford. About the first of September, 1929, I quit my job at the hardware store and returned to Weatherford.

DAD SAM BORDEN

Sam Borden (Whispering Sam)

Dad was Justice of the Peace, Precinct No. 1, Parker County, Texas. His jurisdiction was all of Parker County with the exception of Aledo, Poolville and Springtown. My former partner, Frank Fulgham, took office as District Judge on the same day my Dad took office as Justice of the Peace. After this happened I came to my office the next day and there was a large sign on the door stating "NO COUNTY COURT CASES ACCEPTED". A sign painter friend of mine put it there. After two terms dad had to quit because of bad health. In addition to being a farmer, he also operated a service station on the East side of Weatherford. *(Leon Tanner remembers washing windshields for Mr. Borden at his station for 5 cents per windshield.)* And he also drove a school bus. His route was generally to the east and northeast of Weatherford. He went out toward Aledo and came up to the old Borden Community and the Dicey Community, then maybe he went around to the Wright Community. Charlie Smith, Ed Heathington and Ray Cretsinger all drove buses in the southwest part of the county.

Jack states: Now I don't know about the others, but Sam Borden was the captain of the ship. And what he said on the bus was the law. If the kids got to misbehaving, he might stop the bus and give somebody a spanking right there on the road. Now he had one young fellow who lived over east of Dicey and Clearfork Baptist Church that was full of devilment and he'd sort of drag along.

Dad told him a time or two, "Now son, if you don't get out here when this bus is coming, you're going to be left behind one of these days." This didn't do any good, so one day he kept dragging and Dad just drove off and left him out there. I'm sure his parents gave him a good tanning when he got back to the house and told them what had happened.

Dad did have on accident while driving the bus. There was a little bridge over an old creek across the road between Ed Dill's house and the Clearfork Baptist Church. There came a heavy rain, and dad was driving that bus pretty early that morning and he got on the south end of it before he realized that the north end had fallen into the creek. The story goes that he kept hollering whoa – whoa and pulling back on the steering wheel. He was trying to get that thing stopped . Fortunately, nobody was hurt.

Jack Borden (three years) with dog, Bob, sister Willie and Dad Sam Borden.

AFTER RETURN FROM YUMA AND WEATHERFORD COLLEGE

"Old Main" Weatherford College on South Main St. Torn down when New-Weatherford College was built in 1968

Jack tells that the kids he ran around with at Yuma were making plans to go to University of Arizona, and being with them made him want to go to college. So he moved back to Weatherford and entered Weatherford College. Now in those days you did not have to have a high school diploma or even take an entrance exam.

Jack went on to become a great student at Weatherford College and graduated in spring of 1931. He lettered in Basketball, Track and Football.

In the Oak Leaf for 193l Jack is listed as:
Football 1930 and 193l
Basketball 1930-193l
Track 193l

Annual Picture
Jack Borden- 1931
Weatherford College

Jack Borden- Football
Weatherford College 1931

Jack always did his best (even if he did have flat feet),
and his best helped win many of the games

College Basketball Team- Jack Borden 2nd from left on front row

POPULARITY SOCIETY

Jack has not fully explained about the Popularity Society at Weatherford College, but we feel, since it took up one entire page of the Oak Leaf, that we should mention this.

President Haskell Terry
Vice-President Jack Borden
Chairman Haskell Terry
Treasurer Jack Borden

Committee Members
Jack Borden
Haskell Terry

(At this point we might add that each of these fine young gentlemen are the only members listed)

We quote: The Weatherford Daily Headache states that Hood Wilkins is about to embark upon the Sea of Matrimony in a canoe. Someone said that if Dr. Boger, LLD. ETC., required the ministerial students to pay their tution, so many of them wouldn't get married.

One more bit of information about this Society:

ANNUAL BUDGET

Liabilities $264.25 Assets $233.80

The liabilities included, but not limited to: Cigarettes for Editor, Expenses of Annual Staff, Food to be eaten while at work, Party expenses for Staff and actual expenses of Annual was $200.00.

Assets included but not limited to: Bribes paid to Grind Section, Four pounds of Watermelon seed, Money to influence beauty section, Five hens, one rooster, One used Ford – no value, Parts for Ford $5.00.

(If anyone has information about the above we might file a lawsuit with Borden and Westoff.)

Another item of interest : On Feb. 23, 1931 an item is entered in Important Events as follows: JACK BORDEN arrives at History 7:45, on time, Biggest event of the year.

Jack says: "On our graduation, we had it outside on the west side of the main building. It was late in the afternoon. Here we all sat with our caps and gowns on, waiting for the ceremony to begin. Olene Barnett sat next to me. And a bird flew over. Of course birds have to leave their droppings somewhere. The tassel on my cap was the "somewhere'. Olene looked at it and she looked up. There were couple of buzzards up there. She said "I hope they don't fly over."

Jack has always had a great feeling about Weatherford College. He is one of a handful of people to receive the Carlos Hartnett Award from WC's development foundation, recognizing him in 2000 for going above and beyond the call of duty to bring resources to W. C.

1856- Law Before Jack Borden

THE UNIVERSITY OF TEXAS

THE UNIVERSITY OF TEXAS was the next stop for Jack Borden, the young man who wanted to be a preacher but settled for a lawyer. He graduated from University of Texas Law School in 1936 and immediately moved back to Weatherford. With the exception of a few years with the FBI he has belonged to Parker County ever since.

But one good story— when he entered his second year at University of Texas and first year in law school, Mrs. George Fant lived there and she had a rooming house, sort of boarding house for boys. Her son Knox, now deceased, was in school there. Mrs. Fant asked Jack if he wanted a job. He told her that he would have to have a job- that he needed a job so he could pay room and board. Mrs. Fant explained to Jack that she had a big rooming house with half a dozen boys living there. She told Jack that if he would clean the house, make up the beds and wash the dishes she would give him his room and board. Of course he accepted the job. Now the front of the house was level with the street but the back stood about l0 feet of the ground. She took Jack and showed him the upstairs with the various bathrooms and bedrooms and then downstairs where the kitchen was and then said "Now, Jack I will show you your room." They walked down some wooden stairs to the back yard. A trip Jack says he will never forget. They turned left when they got down the stairs and went through a homemade door. The door opened into a room with a l0 x l0 wooden platform. There was a desk on the platform along with a bed and an overhead pull light. The closet was a piece of wire that ran from one pole to the other where you hung your clothes. All the rest of the room was dirt. Jack said O.K when she said this is your room. Jack moved in and lived there a whole year. The good feature about it was, Jack chewed tobacco and with the dirt floor he didn't have to have a spittoon. He just leaned over and spit over the edge of the platform.

JACK BORDEN

LATER YEARS

TOM WATSON WATERMELON SLICING.
Laud

DISTRICT ATTORNEY JACK BORDEN

Jack Borden was elected District Attorney in 1938. He took office January 1st, 1939. Served a 2 year term, ran again, and served a second term. Terms were 2 years each at that time. However, in March of 1942 he resigned, and after failing to get in the Army because of being color blind, went into the FBI.

He often states that he was District Attorney of Parker County four years and Mayor of Weatherford four years and further adds that the reason he was elected was that he had no opponent either time. You will find many excellent true "tales" of his experiences as DA and Mayor. He left his mark and excellent reputation in both places.

Parker County Courthouse
1886

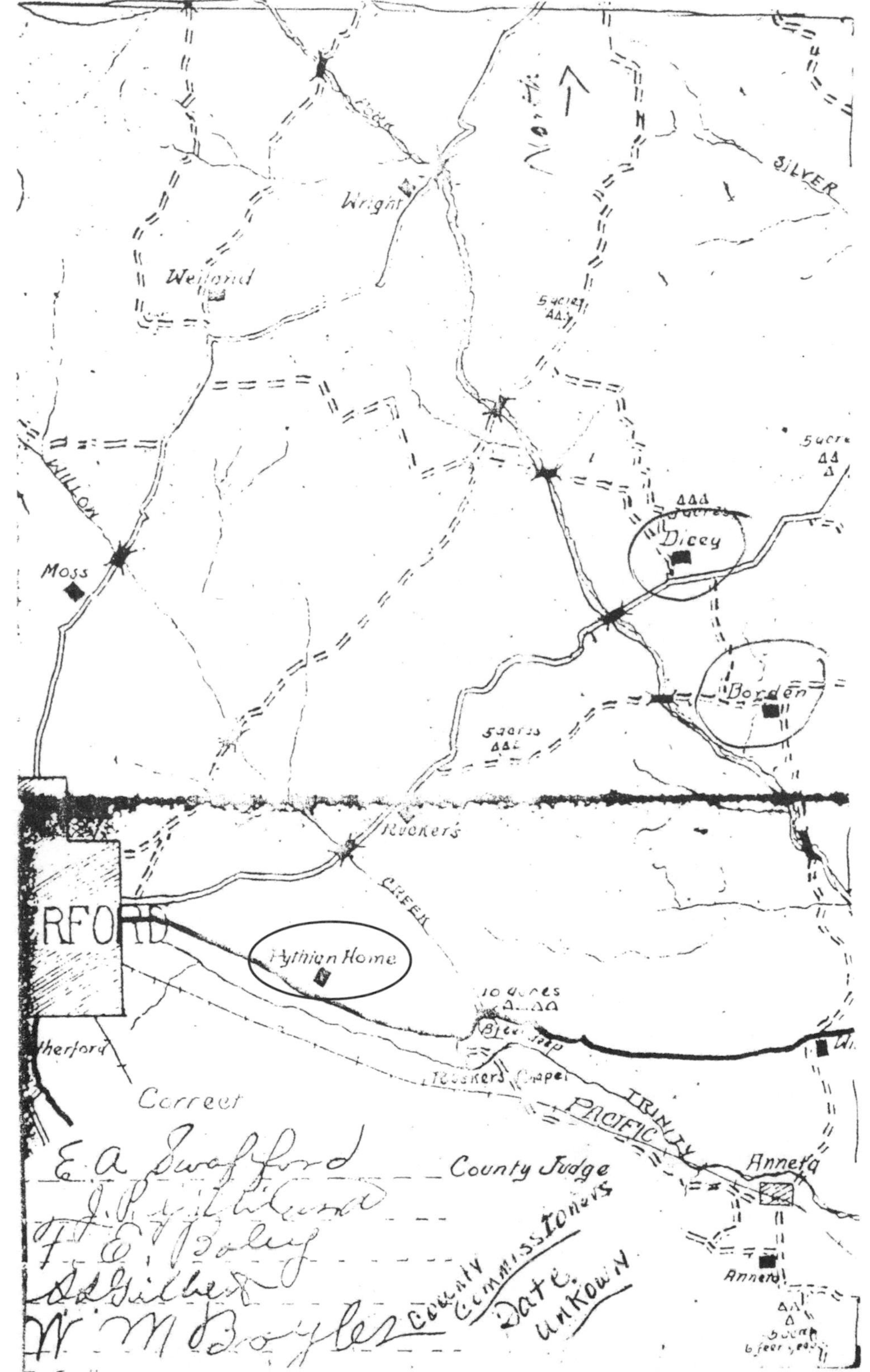
North
Wright
SILVER
Weiland
5 acres
Moss
WILLOW
Dicey
Borden
5 acres
Ruckers
CREEK
RFORD
Pythian Home
10 acres
Rusker's Chapel
TRINITY
PACIFIC
Carreet
County Judge
County Commissioners
Date Unkown
Anneta
W M Boyles

MARRIAGE

Jack and Edith were married in 1940. It was a quiet ceremony with only a little familyand their pastor, Charles T. Whaley of the First Baptist Church present. There was a reason for this. Jack was D. A. at this time and in close contact with his many Highway Patrol friends in the area. Since he and Edith were taking a honeymoon, by car, Jack felt it would stop some "bothering" by his friends who were in charge of the highways. Of course after they were gone, word got out that Jack and Edith were married and there was not much his buddies in the Highway Patrol could do then.

Edith Jordan was the daughter of E.M. Jordan, Sr. and her mother was a James. Her grandfather James ran a stagecoach and stageline from Weatherford to Graham. In fact he finally built a big home in Graham and moved there for good. He hauled both freight and passengers as this was the outpost in the early days. He later sold out at Graham and ended up at a big ranch in northeastern New Mexico.

Edith's father was in the grocery business on North Main St. in the early days. It was called Jordan's Grocery and it is said that her mother would answer the phone at the grocery store as "Jurdan's Grocery" Mrs. Jordan speaking. Mr. Jordan died before Edith and Jack married.

Jack states: "Edith had her Masters Degree and was teaching school when we were married in 1940. In those days, married women were not allowed to teach in Weatherford School District because it was right at the end of the Great Depression and it was said the men needed the jobs. So she had to quit teaching in Weatherford. However, this did not stop her and she went to teaching in Peaster as they had lost some teachers due to the war.

A story while she was teaching at Peaster. Jack was D. A. at the time and the highway patrol officers always hung out in his office. One day a big ice storm came up and the roads were bad. Some of the officers were loafing in the D.A.'s office and Jack decided they needed to go to work and he needed help. He asked the two guys if they were just loafing and they replied "Yeah". Jack then told or ask them to go to Peaster where his wife worked and one of them drive her car back. When the highway patrol officers arrived in their marked cars and ask for Mrs. Edith Borden, those kids eyes got very big. It seemed that years later some of her students commented about the day "The Highway Patrol" came for their teacher.

EDITH BORDEN AND LAW

"Old Bell" moved from "Old Main" to present Weatherford College

After Jack and Edith returned from the FBI, Edith started teaching at Weatherford College. And Jack states: "Oh Lord a mercy, I don't think she made over $100 per month or something like that. We were having a woman to come to the house and cook lunch and keep the house everyday. When I explained to her that we were losing money and I thought she might as well quit", she replied "Well, if I can study law? I ask if she meant go to law school. She explained that she had her Master's Degree and was eligible to take the Bar if she did a certain number of hours of study. I told her to go for it and I didn't pay any attention until one day she ask if she could go to Austin and take the cram course and the law exam. She said it was a couple of weeks off and I told her to go ahead.

She went down to Austin and stayed a week, or maybe a little longer. She took the cram course and passed the bar exam with better grades than 90 percent of those who had graduated from a college law school. She got her license to practice law in 1962. She was the first Parker County woman licensed to practice law.

She never did practice law, but she took up substitute teaching. Her friend, Wilma Grace Buchanan, was teaching and her mother was quite ill. When Wilma Grace had to be out with her mother, Edith was called in to substitute. She also substituted for many other teachers. They finally relaxed the rule and married women were allowed to teach but she never did go back to fulltime teaching.

During her substitute days the McDavid Boys and the two boys of Lloyd Smith stand out in my mind. They were full of mischief and I heard a lot about them.

Mrs. Jack Borden Named
"Teacher of the Year"
By
Pioneer District Federation of Women's Clubs

Jack *(1961)* *Edith*

FBI DAYS OF JACK BORDEN

Jack was in Weatherford when the Japanese bombed Pearl Harbor. He decided to join the Army . However fate was changed by the physicians at San Antonio. He was color blind and turned away. A good friend of his at Camp Wolters recommended that he join the FBI and his service could be utilized in that manner. Jack was acquainted with the Agent in charge of the FBI's Dallas office. He got in touch with the Agent in charge known as SAC and explained that Jack wanted an application for admittance in the FBI. Some three weeks after the application was mailed back Jack received notification that Jack had been accepted and to report to Washington D.C. in ten days. When he left the FBI he was 37 years old and there was nowhere in the world he wanted to be more than Weatherford where he grew up. He was back home one more time.

JEFFERSON DAVIS

IS DEAD.

A Public Meeting will be held at the Courthouse this, Saturday, evening at 7 o'clock, to adopt suitable resolutions expressive of the deep sorrow that fills the hearts of the people. All are invited, and the Ladies are especially requested to be present.

M. W. BUSTER,
Mayor City of Weatherford.

Weatherford, Dec. 7, 1889.

Constitution Print.

(We bet Jack is glad he was not in the FBI at this time)

(Also notice ladies are welcome)

PARKER COUNTY

Old Settlers Picnic and Reunion

IS TO BE HELD AT HOLLAND'S LAKE

WEATHERFORD, TEXAS

Thursday, Aug. 8, 1929

Everybody Invited

This is to be an old style basket picnic. Fill the basket with grub and come along. Coffee furnished at the grounds. Everybody invited to come and enjoy the day.

Finest collection of historical relics of Parker County and Southwest. Interesting talks. Address by Hon. R. B. Hood, who knows the history of this county, as few persons do, at 11 o'clock. Old time fiddle music by Ed Glenn's Fiddle Band of Throckmorton, Texas.

Come. Bring your friends. Holland's Lake is a delightful place to hold a picnic—trees, shade and water.

See how the first settlers used to live—the guns they used, tools, utensils, clothing, etc. Hear the old pioneers tell of the times and experiences that will be no more.

Everybody Welcome

(In 1937 or 1938 Jack Borden was the principal speaker)

WHY PRACTICE LAW

Jack has been asked many times how he decided to become a lawyer. He states that he always thought the next thing to a preacher was a lawyer or a doctor. For reasons given elsewhere in this book, concerning a cat, he decided to be a lawyer rather than a preacher. At the time he graduated from the University of Texas School of Law, he firmly believed that doctors and lawyers were just a shade below pastors in the respect of the community. And Jack says he still believes that, except he readily admits that all three categories have slipped some, and particularly lawyers.

Jack states: "All the times I've practiced law, I've tried to do what I believed when I got out of law school, and that is that you are here to serve the people. My primary interest in my clients has been, not the fee that I'm going to get, but what I could do to take care of their problems. That's been primary, the fee has been secondary. Over the years my partners often made the remark to me that I gave away more than I took in. To my knowledge, I've never had a written contract with any client, whereby we agree I'll do so-and-so and they'll pay so-and-so. I just told them, here's what we'll do, and they say, OK, and that's it."

Jack says he has never asked anybody to give him a part of a fee in advance. When the work was done, he presented the bill. He further states that not more than a half a dozen times in 67 years have either one of them failed to do what they had agreed to do. When people were poor and he felt they might not be able to pay, he, in a few instances, did ask for court cost in advance.

Jack has been representing families for four generations. A lady in his office just the other day acknowledged that Jack had represented her grandfather, her father, and was the only lawyer she had ever had and now he is representing her daughter. She has a 5 year old grandson that she wanted me to do some legal work for so she could tell people I had been the family lawyer for five generations.

Pythian Home- Jack has been a member of K.P. Lodge over 60 years

MAYOR OF WEATHERFORD

The first "mayor" story jack tells is probably remembered by many. Jack says: Well, most people run for mayor to help out their town. When I announced for mayor, the main reason I did so, was I had a friend, Raymond Anderson, who was long time meter man for the City of Weatherford. Now Raymond was very considerate and if he saw a meter expired and the owner of the vehicle was in the business, he'd just tap on the door or window and point to the meter. They would go drop a nickel in the meter and he would move on to the next meter.

Well, the powers that be, they didn't like that and they had Raymond on the carpet a time or two about it. Raymond did not stop and finally they just demoted him and put him back in the repair shop. That sort of irritated me because Raymond was my good friend and I knew he was doing a great job. I talked to some of the higher ups and it didn't do any good.

When the Mayor's job was up, I just went up and announced. I got elected because I didn't have an opponent. I didn't have enough friends on the commission the first term of two years, but I was patient. The next term I got all my friends on the City Commission. One of the first things we did was to remove the cause of Raymond being taken of the meters and put in the repair shop. He returned to the meters and stayed their until he retired. My main job was done and I was ready to quit, but I went ahead and served out my second term. The two terms ran 1960 to 1964.

Raymond Anderson

The second "mayor" story is as follows and is called his "near impeachment".

There was a lady that came just before Christmas time to ask the City Commission for a permit to shoot fireworks in town. She lived where it was vacant all around her, and a little creek nearby, and her boys just loved fireworks. We told her no because there was a city ordinance that said that you could not shoot fireworks in town, it was a violation of the law. The woman was in tears, but finally started to leave. She got nearly out the back door and I spoke up and said "Lady, come back up here". She came back and I told her a little story. I told her I knew exactly how she felt, because I had a friend down underneath the hill from me that had two little boys, and like her little boys, they love fireworks. I explained that these little boys come up to my house on 4th of July and Christmas when everyone shoots fireworks. Now there's a big vacant lot behind me, nobody there, and no close neighbors. Jack further told the lady that "These little boys and I go out there and shoot fireworks until we think the police are nearly there, then we run in the house, turn the lights out and lock the doors." The lady thanked me and left. Jack said he thought they were going to impeach him. But he states that he was honest and that is exactly what he and the boys did.

Because of this incident it is Jack's belief that an ordinance was approved wherein a person could get a permit to shoot fireworks in town if you did not live too close to anybody and an adult was there to supervise the fireworks.

TRAVEL

Jack says when he became 70 years old, or there about, he decided it was time to do a little traveling. Edith had been to Europe a couple of times and they had been over most of the United States, with Red River being one of their favorite spots. It was time to get out of the US.

Their first trip was in 1968 when they went with the Law Group to Italy, and Greece. Among other cities were Rome and Athens. On this trip they were on a cruise trip and visited most of the Greek Islands including Crete, Mikanos, St. John, Patmos, and one stop in Turkey. After the cruise they flew to Frankfort, Germany and then home. They had been bit by the travel bug.

The year 2002 was the first year in 53 years the Borden's did not go to Red River, New Mexico, on account of Edith's health. In the late 1970's they started traveling. In the next 20 years they traveled to a large part of the world and Jack says it is a long way from a farm on the Clear Fork to China, Norway, Sweeden, Greece, Italy and other countries in between.

One trip they have made, with good friends, Boley and Evelyn Pearson, for 21 consecutive years has been to Lake Tahoe on the Nevada –California line.

We will end the travels of Jack Borden with a very interesting story as only Jack can tell. This trip was to Patmos. Now if you remember in the Bible, John's Grotto, where he wrote Revelations, was on Patmos, says Jack. There's a beautiful Greek Orthodox church at the very top, with gold and all that stuff. There was only three ways to get up there. You could walk, you could take a bus, or you could ride a mule. Being an old time cowboy, Jack decided he would ride the mule. There were a bunch of lawyers on that trip and one of Jack's lawyer friends said "Why, it's the first time in my life I've ever seen one jackass riding another jackass."

Jack, Edith, Evelyn and Boley
Flagstaff, Arizona 1993

RELIGION

Jack tells the story of why he was not a preacher. It seems a cat and his mother had a lot to do with it. Originally Jack says he was going to be a Baptist preacher. However, and incident happened that changed his mind.

Jack stated: "My Mother had just finished churning. That was one of the old churns where you had a dasher that you churned up and down with. It was about a three –gallon churn, I guess. When she finished churning and had taken the butter out, she left the lid off. She heard me say "I baptize you in the name of the Holy Ghost". When she turned around she saw that I had just stuck my black cat all the way to the bottom of that full churn of fresh buttermilk. Well, the after-effects were such that every time I thought about baptism, I got to hurting. If I had been a Methodist, or knew something about sprinkling, I'd have probably been a preacher." Jack doesn't remember what happened to the cat – only what happened to him. Anyway the buttermilk was ruined.

ON CHURCH – Jack stated: "I have been a Baptist for some 82 years. I made a confession of faith and was baptized in the Clear Fork, right close to where the power plant is now, and I became a member of the Clearfork Baptist Church . My grandmother was a charter member of the Clearfork Baptist Church.

I left my membership there until I got out of law school, and in 1936 I became a member of the First Baptist Church in Weatherford. I've been a member there ever since, over 62 years. I am a Deacon, and I've been chairman of the Board of Deacons and I taught a Sunday school Class for 25 years or more. I am the president of the class now, and the main reason I am is that they say, "We'll not have an election because he's got a certain amount of talk he's gonna have to do. So let's get it over with so we can have a Sunday school lesson." That's the kind of respect they have for old folks. There is only one member of the class older them me – that is Obie Beene – he is 103 years old.

Although I have devoted most of my time to the practice of Law, I have always believed that but for the Grace of God and his help I would not have been able to do the things I have done. I thank him daily. I am more proud of trying to do something for a Church or Churches than of my success as a "Country Lawyer". It makes me feel that I am repaying a part of what God has done for me.

Some might say I did my church work for devious reasons on grounds that they helped me. And according to that, I might say that I was trying a lawsuit against a Fort Worth or Dallas lawyer, I've forgotten which, and the judge instructed the jurors, all of them men at that time, that although we might be very good friends with some of the jurors, they couldn't carry on fraternizing or carry on any conversations with any of the attorneys involved in the case. That it's all right to say, "Good Morning" or "Good afternoon", and whatnot, but you're not supposed to carry on any conversations. We had a recess, and the lawyer from out of town and I was walking down a hallway and one of the jurors walked up to me and said, "Jack, could I say something to you?" I told him – no – because the judge had admonished us that we cannot talk with each other. Well, he said "Surely he won't care if I tell you how much my church appreciates all the work you have done for them and did not charge anything." As we walked further down the hall and turned a corner, the lawyer says to me : "Is there any way we can settle this lawsuit?"

In another case I was trying, before I quit trying divorces, I was trying a divorce suit for some good friends of mine. My friends were Baptists, and their daughter was a Baptist who I represented. It was over custody of a minor child. We had some good old Baptist women at the First Baptist Church, and Laura Light (Mrs. Harvey Light) was really the leader of these women.

They stayed in the witness room the entire time of this trial – praying constantly. It so happened that the defendant, the father of the child, had his mother there to testify as a witness in his behalf. After we got through with all our witnesses, they called his mother as a witness. Now Laura Light had already pulled me off to the side and informed me that she thinks the mother feels it is the best interest of the child for the mother to have it. As this mother was examined by her son's attorney she told the jury what a fine man her son was and then they turned her over to me. I first ask her was she a Christian and she replied yes. I then ask her if she ever prays and she said she did. I inquired as to whether or not she had prayed about who should have custody of this child and she stated that she had. I then ask her if, down deep in her heart, did she believe that the best interest of this child would be if the court awarded custody to the mother. She replied, "I sure do." Needless to say, the jury awarded custody of the child to the mother. Now this lawyer, who was on the other side went back to Fort Worth and told all his friends that, if you ever try a lawsuit over in Parker County against Jack Borden, be sure his client's not a Baptist, because if you do, they'll pray you out of court.

Another Church experience was at the Texas Café. One day Byron Patrick, a good friend of mine, and I were talking when I was prosecuting attorney. Now being in the position I was in, I tried to be pretty careful about the kind of life I was living. Byron made the statement "Jack, you remind me of a preacher's son." Of course I ask why and he said, "I just keep waiting for you to break out and do what you would like to do."

Jack Bordens Church Awards

First Baptist Church of Weatherford- In the early days. Jack has been a member since 1936

AROUND THE PARKER COUNTY COURTHOUSE SQUARE

THE OLD TIN WATERMELON

When Jack Borden thinks of the old tin watermelon that set on the southeast corner of the square he very quickly remembers something that happened when he was prosecuting attorney. It seems the Chief of Police or Sheriff or somebody had brought a couple of young boys in about l3 or 14 years old.

Now these boys were runaways, came from New Jersey of New York or somewhere way off. When Jack asked the boys where they spent the night, they just sort of looked at each other. Of course Jack encouraged them to tell the truth. They finally admitted that they spent the night in the old tin watermelon on the square. Many will remember the old watermelon with a big square cutout place in the top. Jack, or it seems, no one else knows what happened to the watermelon. If the boys are alive today, they probably remember it and do not really care what happened to it.

AROUND THE SQUARE AND MORE

Jack states that he has known Weatherford since he was a little kid. However he says they did not come to town very often since they lived eight miles east of town. The only mode of transportation was horse and buggy and they ordinarily did not come to town except when necessary

He further states that he well remembers coming to town with a load of watermelons and parking out there on the square. A lot of pictures you see around of those days – well Jack might be in some of them.

The courthouse then was a little different than it is now, and the sheriff's office at that time was on the south side and you would go in the south door and turn to the left and there was the sheriff's office.

Looking down South Main on your left, which would have been east of South Main, Mr. J. B. Alvis bought watermelons and cotton out of that place at one time. When Jack got out of Law School, Pat Jordan had Ashland's Ice Cream, a great big old place there in the middle of that block. Not long after he got back from law school, Lester Stewart said to Jack one day: "Hey, let's go over to Pat's and get us an ice cream." Sounded good to Jack so they went. Now Pat had a light switch with the old cord that you'd pull down and the button to pull it down with was six feet off the ground. Pat would say that if anyone can kick that button, "I'll give them all the ice cream they can eat, it'll all be free." The button was half-way between the front door and the fountain to the back. Lester said: "Pat, I've got somebody and I'll bet you a quarter against all the ice cream that I can eat that he can kick that button." Of course Pat said you're on. Lester just pulled his pocket knife out, cut the cord, and dropped the button on the floor and Jack kicked it. They both got all the ice cream they could eat. The last time Jack ever saw old Pat he was still complaining.

The Nook Café was there in the middle of the block and Frank Dore's tire shop was on the east side of Pat's ice cream place. The gas company was there on the corner just across from Cotten Bratten. A stairway went up above the corner building where the Abstract Company was. There was two Abstract Companies, Brown and W. D. Taylor. One was the Parker County Abstract and the other was Weatherford Abstract.

Now on the corner up stairs over the gas company was where Preston Martin had his law office. There was a stairway that went up about the middle of the block where Preston Martin walked up to his office. Ben Hagman married his daughter, Mary Martin, and he officed with Preston Martin.

On the corner across from the Martin offices was and still

is, the Cotten Bratton Furniture Store and Funeral Parlor. I knew Uncle Dave Bratton and Fred Cotten quite well as I do Virginia Cotten Scott and James Cotten.

Now just north of the Cotten furniture store, was later Prichard's Grocery Store. There was another store there earlier but? Going on north, Andy Brinkley owned and operated what was later the Peter's Café. On the corner of Ft. Worth St. just north of Peter's Café was Glenn Bros. Grocery and later John L. Heartsill Tire Store.

Skipping over Ft. Worth St., on the corner was the First National Bank. Up stairs was the McCall's law office. There was a F. W. Woolworth store that later becamc Duke and Ayres. Up stairs was Shropshire and Bankhead Law Offices and Mr. Gatlin ran the Texas Business College up there also. Next came Victor Scherer's Hardware with the Firestone Store next. Mr. Lawrence Edwards owned a store in there somewhere – you know he was Mildred Beards father. Burette Hobson also had a tire store on the corner, maybe before Heartsill or the Firestone. Pope Puryear ran the corner store for quite some time.

Parker County's 3rd Courthouse

SIDEWALK LITTER

The City filed a criminal case against a client of Jacks for littering. He was displaying his merchandise on the street in violation of a City Ordinance. He and Jack checked the streets and found that one of the City Commissioners had a pair of scales that cost a penny to weigh, which penny went to the Commissioner. On the sidewalk in front of his business another Commissioner had tires displayed on a side street. Jack's client gave him the money to pay the fine. Jack took it to the City Judge. The next day Jack sent his client to the City Hall to file charges against the two Commissioners for littering. This caused quite a stir with City Fathers and the municipal judge called Jack and said "Hey, we need to settle this thing some way." Jack said; "Well, give the man you first filed on his money back." The judge said you gave me the check and if you'll come up here I'll just give you a check." Jack Borden said: "No, I walked and brought the check to you, and I expect you to walk and bring it back to me." The Judge brought the check right down. Case dismissed.

BACK TO THE SQUARE

There was a drug store on the next block where Davis City Pharmacy is today. Scarlett Drug was there in the early days and others have owned a drug store there. On the corner, across Whiskey Alley (Austin Ave.) was the Kendell Building. Ralph Kendell had an automovile agency there. There were two Kendell's – R. W. was a druggist and he was the father of Mrs. Willard Saddler. There was a basement under the Kendell Building. There was a beauty shop down there and my wife opened up a gift shop there called-Open House. Later on Ruby Jones bought my wife out and moved it up on the west side of the square.

Now down north on Whiskey Alley and Spring Street was the Wagon Yard – Once Lovelady and then Kemp from 1920 on until 1945. On the east side of the street between Kendells and the Wagon Yard was the Chambers Meat Market and at one time Claude and Kit Thomas ran a restaurant there. There was a rooming house on Spring St. just across the street from the Wagon Yard ran by Silas Kemp and family. Most of the businesses on North Main Street in the first two blocks went all the way to Whiskey Alley and operated out of their back doors for deliveries.

Hart Grocery and Carter Ivy Hardware opened on North Main and had back doors on Whiskey Alley. Carter Ivy is still there today. Now there was a little barbershop sort of in the alley off of North Main. The Doughety's had built the place in an alley and Peanut Martin was the barber there. Now Peanut was in the café one day and somebody was making some disparaging remarks about Mr. Doughety. And Peanut took up for him. He said: "He's the best landlord I've ever had. If I don't take him the rent on the first day of the month or the second day of the month, he comes down here and gets it."

A lot of people still remember the Texas Café on the West side of the present Davis City Pharmacy. The Patrick Family owned and operated it, oh, maybe a hundred years, maybe. In fact when they decided to close it, they couldn't find the key. I guess Byron had died and it was open 24 hours a day 7 days a week. Who needed a key.

DELIVERING ICE WITH JACK AND MULE

Jack relates a story concerning he and Mule Kaiser and the Texas Café. Jack delivered ice in the residential section of town and Mule, a big guy, delivered to business houses. Now Jack and Mule wanted to go somewhere on a Saturday, so Jack helped Mule. Mule was about 6 ft. 2 and weighed around 200 lbs. Jack was 5 ft. 11 and if he was wet he might weigh in at 160 lbs. They drove up to the Texas Café with blocks of ice that weighed 300 lbs. Mule opened up the back end and cut one of those blocks of ice half in to. He put 150 on his back and went into the Texas Café. Now Jack says he thought he could do anything that Mule Kaiser could and he put 150 lbs on his back just like Mule did. When Jack came out of the café, Mr. Patrick, Byron's dad, stopped him and said "Now son, I watched you go through here and I figured that those legs would have to give away on you at any time. Now, if that big Mule wants to carry 150 pounds, you let him do it. But don't you be carrying 150 pounds." Jack did just as Mr. Patrick said – never again.

BACK TO THE SQUARE

Beyond The Texas Café was Crowder's Barber Shop. Ike Simmons' brother, Charlie, was a custodian and shined shoes there. Jack states that he always got his hair cut there because L. J. Crowder was the owner of the shop and usually cut his hair free. When Jack went into the FBI, it was 18 months before he got back, and the first person he saw and shook hands with in the barbershop was Charlie Simmons. He was Jacks very good friend.

Jack goes on to say that we had a bunch of good black people in Weatherford, all his friends. Of course there were some, just like white people, who would get over the edge occasionally. But for the most part they were just really fine people. There were people like Allison Pickard, the Gratts family and the Ruckers along with the Simmons' who were some of the greatest people you could find anywhere.

TIME FOR A TALE

Now, Charlie's uncle, one of Ike's boys, was named Tom. It seems that Tom had a little habit of getting into some little trouble ever so often. Jack tells that Tom came up to his office while he was prosecuting attorney and said: "Mr. Jack, I'm going to take a trip to California and could you write me a letter of recommendation?" When Jack asked him if he could tell him anything good about himself, Tom replied: "Well now, Mr. Jack, you know me pretty well." Jack called his secretary and asked for a copy of a letter of recommendation he had prepared for Ross Robertson a few days ago. Jack asked her to remove Ross Robertson's name from the letter and insert Tom Simmons and Jack signed it and sent Tom on his way. When Tom got back from California he visited with Jack and said: "Mr. Jack, everywhere I'd go with that letter, they'd say, Hey, you must be a good man." Fine man

BACK TO THE SQUARE

After the barbershop was a drugstore, an old Rexall Drugstore. Dr. MacNelly and Dr. Simmons had their offices upstairs inside that building. I don't know who operated that drugstore at the time, but it was later Wren's Rexall. Next to that was the old Merchants and Farmers State Bank. In the basement, there was a barber shop and Jim Plumlee was a barber down there. Jack thinks Slim Bruce was a barber there also. There were some offices upstairs sometimes used by Realtors.

On the corner of North Main and the square was the Citizens National Bank – Now Weatherford National Bank. The bank occupied about a half or a third of what it occupies now. Jack's first recollection of a president at the bank is Mr. G. A. Holland. He was president for many years and then Fred Smith succeeded him. After Fred, Jim Campbell, and then J. W. Ford maybe was after him. Mr. Holland was a great friend of Jack's as were the others.

Upstairs, Grindstaff, Zellers and Hutcheson had their law firm and it was a real fine law firm. They did work all over the state and were real good in worker's compensation cases. J. D. and Lloyd Doughety had an office up stairs as did V. P. Craven. V. P. got a little busier than he wanted to be one time, so he put a sign on the outside of his door that said, "No new business is taken in until I get rid of what I've got." And that was V. P. He just did what he wanted to do.

They were all real fine lawyers. Mr. Grindstaff never had any children and Mr. Hutcheson never had any children. Mr. A. E. Zellers had one son, Austin, and he had a son, Eddie, and he practices law today. But that's all that's left of that law firm.

Going down North Main from the present day Texas Bank, if I'm not mistaken, a man by the name of Baouvestt, he was a Frenchman, had a restaurant along there. On the rest of the street, I don't remember much except Carter-Ivy Hardware and its still there. Jack Hart's grocery was next to the hardware store on the corner. There was a tire store along there somewhere, run by R. B. Gibson's Uncle George. It was across Spring St. and beyond was Milburn Hardware Store. Then you could go all the way down to Bridge Street and across Bridge was C. D. Hartnett as it is today. There was a motor repair shop there and a Mr. Miers had a repair shop there. There was a rooming house somewhere along there and that is where Wheeler Hardin and some of the fellows lived. On the West side of North Main was the Jordan Grocery. Mr. Jordan was my wife, Edith's, father. Edith's mother is the one who would answer the phone "Jurdans Grocery" – Mrs. Jordan speaking.

SPRINKLING THE DUST

One day I saw the street sweeper coming along the street and it was squirting a little water out. What I remember is that my grandmother lived over on Bridge Street and they had a wagon with a big ole tank on it pulled by some horses. They sprinkled the streets to keep the dust down. Instead of the street sweepers, they had "street wetters."

In the name and by the authority of

The State of Texas

To all to whom these presents shall come — Greeting:
Know ye, that

JACK BORDEN

is hereby commissioned

Admiral

in the

Texas Navy

with all rights and privileges appertaining thereto and with the duty of ...sisting in the preservation of the history, boundaries, water resources, and civil defense of the State.

In testimony whereof, I have hereunto signed my name and caused the Seal of the State to be affixed at the City of Austin, this the 10th *day of* April *A.D.* 1963.

JOHN CONNALLY, Governor

"Coming on up toward the courthouse was the old Waldroms store. I.B. Hand and I bought this building in 1960, remodeled it completely and practiced law from the building from the middle of 1960 to Setember, 2000. The building is now named Borden and Hand Building.

In September, 2000, John built the building we now occupy at 1250 Santa Fe Drive, Weatherford, Texas . I.B. decided he no longer cared to practice law and did not move with us. He does have an office in the Texas Bank."

JACK CONTINUES UP NORTH MAIN

Coming on up North Main, after Waldrom's, Pharo and James had a grocery store and before that George Kelly had a drug-store right in there. Kelly had a fountain and everything. And I think, Bartholds had a little clothing store. Not long ago there was still the inscription on the building that said "Barthold". Of course we have already talked about the Citizens bank on the corner. There were two theaters, Palace and Princess. There was a barbershop on the east side of the Palace and a jewelry store on the west side of the entrance. Dorothy Watt was the owner at one time and then it was Thelma Hayden.

Then Gernsbacker had a five-and-dime store and later a part of that building was occupied by Gilbert's clothing store. Jenkins Dry Goods was on the corner where the Hub is today. Cross over York Ave. and there was the Baker Posten Store, later it was W. H. Bowdens and Sons. When I knew the Bowdens, Ed Bowden and I were good friends, the Bowdens lived up above the store. There was Andy, Lon, Elmer (We called him Bid) and Edgar. Just below the old Bowden store was the "Daily Herald." Mr. Al MacNelly owned the paper and Mr. A. A. Patrick was the reporter and editor for many years. Andrew Colgin had a cleaning place right next door to the Herald Office. Going South across Dallas Ave. to the corner on the square was J. C. Penny's store. I worked there when I was in college. Katy Kirkpatrick was a long time worker at Penny's. I don't think the J. C. Penny building belonged to the Kutemans as did the south side of that block. I am not sure who owned the north end of the Kuteman block but that is where the Opera House was in the old old days. Corcanges Drug was somewhere in the middle of the block. There was a stairway from the sidewalk up to the second floor and there is where Mr. Nolen Queen and Mr. R. B. Hood had their law office. Now, there was a third floor and they had a large ballroom up there. They had dances and I went to many a dance there. I never will forget, I was up there one night and Lenora White was up there. Lenora must have been 15 or 16, and Ford was her older brother. When we finished the dance, I said "Little girl, do your parents know you're up here?" Since I was quite a bit older than her, I felt comfortable asking her that. She replied: "Well, I"ll have you know my parents do know and my brother's up here with me." She was a spunky little thing. Lenora later became wife of Morris Sands- Mike Sands is their son. Yeah, we had lots of dances up there. Later on the upstairs became apartments and were rented out. The Parker County State Bank was on the corner of the Kuteman Building at one time. I think it was later merged with the Citizens Bank. After the bank, there was a Safeway Store on the corner, and maybe a rcstaurant before that. When the Kuteman building burned in 1951 the Safeway Store and Corcanges and Sturges Allen Ladies Dress Shop were all there.

After the fire, Sturges Allen moved across Palo Pinto Street to the corner. I can't remember what was there before Sturges but John Bradford owned the building. I remember two or three who worked there. Mrs. Bozelle ran the place and Mrs. Orville Milburn and a young Peter Morgan worked there. Now the workers all thought Peter was the greatest fellow there ever was. He is now associated with George, Morgan and Sneed, PC. Others in the block included Mr. Richards with a sports and bicycle shop. And long long ago Joe Wren had a small drug store there. These stores were along where Bowman's and Accent Florist are now. Then a set of stairs left the side-walk and went up to the Knights of Pythias Lodge Hall. That is where all the Pythian meetings were held and other activities. The K. P. Lodge also had an office downstairs on the south side of the stairway. Then on the corner was Sharpe's Grocery for many years. Today, Bennetts Office Supply occupies the old Sharpe Grocery and the K. P. Office Building.

(Editor: I have found out these past few months that there is not much about this town that Jack Borden does not know. Now I know he remembers everything he ever knew, but perhaps he never knew about an elevator at the K. P. Lodge Hall. When I inquired if he knew there was an elevator that you enter just inside the back south door of the lodge hall going behind the old Sharpe's Grocery, he said he never heard of it. Well, thanks to Doyle and Vernell Hutcheson, I know one thing that Jack doesn't.

The story goes: When Leonard Brothers went out of business in Fort Worth many years ago they sold all their equipment and fixtures. Gus Vincent talked to Doyle and said the K. P. lodge hall needed an elevator and they could buy one from Leonard Bros.- and they did just that. For years now, many Pythians enter through the south door and go up in an elevator. Jack Borden, they invite you to take a ride anytime. Mary)

BACK TO THE SQUARE

Now we cross W. Church to the corner where the two Bloom brothers, Harry and Earnest, were in business for many years at this location. They were both dentist and they had another brother, also a dentist. The corner building is gone and it is now a parking lot. The second building still stands today.

Up the street from the Bloom buildings was the Montfort Hotel. Mr. Hunter, father of Mrs. Frank Dore, lived there. A lot of men, either widowers or old bachelors, lived in this hotel. If you go back to the Bloom buildings and go south you will find White's Funeral Home. Mr. W. A. White was the main man for many years. This is the perfect place for one of Jack's stories.

"One time there was quite a storm in Weatherford. The White's put their hearses in a building that was north of where the funeral home is now. The storm caused the roof or the opening to go down. It lacked about three inches being high enough to get the hearses out. Mr. White was quite worried how he was going to get them out. Joe Quante came along and looked the situation over and said to Mr. White "Mr. White, for 25 dollars, I'll get them out of there without a scratch." Mr. White told him to go ahead and get them out. All Joe did was just go and let the air out of the tires, and he drove them out. Mr. White paid him the twenty-five dollars."

BACK TO THE SOUTH SIDE OF SQUARE

Where Colonial Art Shop is today most of us remember Hamilton's Tire Store. Before that however, Walter Varner had a car business. Jack bought his first car there and he gave him a hundred dollars for it, on credit. It was one that Fred Cotten had used, he mostly used it to funerals and back. Now on the driver's side, why, all the paint was off the doors. When Jack asked what happened to the paint on the door, Mr. Varner replied: "Mr. Cotten chews tobacco, and he didn't get it all the way out in the street sometimes. That tobacco juice took the paint off the side." But it was a real good car.

Next was the White Star Laundry. Man, you'd go there in the summertime and that heat would knock you off your feet. In the real old days the next lot was occupied by Todd Monuments. Mrs. Todd was Dr. Campbell's daughter. The Todd"s later owned the building where John Kirkpatrick has had the abstract office for years. We bought that building from Mrs. Todd.

Next was W. D. Taylor Abstract Office where Texas Butane is today. Then Howard Rea Drug was on the corner where the Downtown Café is now. Old pictures show the Rea Drug building being occupied by Weatherford Drug.

OLD PICTURES

AROUND THE SQUARE

WEATHERFORD, TEX.
1925
JACK VENABLE

North East Corner of Square Early 1900-Scarlett Pharmacy is now the location of Davis City Pharmacy

Looking North East from Courthouse

Looking West to Courthouse from Ft. Worth St-Early 1900 Watermelons going to Train Depot.

U.S. Post Office converted to District Court Building in 1990's

Public market ater it was moved from the courthouse square-(Chester Ward)

Chambers meat market Whiskey Alley

Palace and Princess Theaters-North West Side of Square. The Weatherford National Bank now covers this area.

North West corner of courthouse square

Kuteman Building corner of PaloPinto and York Ave.

Old Kuteman Building burning 1951

Looking north from courthouse square down york ave. Late-1800

D.M. Hart Grocery 303 N. Main about 1916

Montfort Hotel-Burning on W. Church St.

Believed to be J.B. Alvis store on south east side of square early 1900

Courthouse Officials- 1936-1940 Tom Erwin, Judge; Wade Hutcheson, Commissioner; Tom Young, Prec. 4 Commissioner; Lester Stewart, Sheriff; Dan Nelson, Commissioner Prec. 3; Victor Scherer, Co. Clerk; and Robert Boyd, Commissioner.

Old-Time Doctors

Dr. Campbell, he may have delivered me, I don't know. I was born out there on Clear Fork. But I had pneumonia when I was about six or seven years old, and they had Dr. MacNelly and Dr. McKenzie, old-time doctors there, and they wanted to operate for some reason, and Dr. Campbell wouldn't allow them to. And so he stayed with me. He practically lived at our house, and got me through that pneumonia.

And I got real bad one night, and telephone lines were all down and it was raining. Clyde Boley was teaching school at Borden School (Boley Pearson's uncle), and Clyde walked that eight miles to town to get a hold of Dr. Campbell to get him to go out there. He was great.

But when my last doctor died, Dr. Ripley, I started looking for a doctor, and I was recommended to talk to somebody at the hospital, you know, being employees up there. And the lady said, "Well, who have your doctors been?"

"Well, I started out with Dr. Campbell."

"Well, I don't believe I've ever heard of him," she said.

And I said, "He's the one the hospital is named after."

But back in the old days, there was Dr. MacNelly and Dr. McKenzie and Dr. Chandler and Dr. Campbell. And then, later on, Dr. Thompson, Case Thompson's father, was the doctor here.

Dr. Fike came in here later. Interesting, interesting old gentleman. I used him on drunk driver cases when I was a prosecutor, and he would examine them and he made an excellent witness. And, you know, he has a granddaughter who lives here. Her name is Forbes. Well, anyhow, Dick Forbes' wife.

I told her this, and she didn't remember it. But I remember Dr. Fike telling me that he started out as more or less a roustabout in a circus and that he might have been an acrobat, too.

But he had the desire to study medicine, and he just went up East or somewhere and managed one way or the other to get a license to practice medicine. He came in here many years after the others.

After Dr. Fike came, Dr. Russell, Dr. Allen and Dr. Funk came. And then Merrick and Smith and Whalen came in. Dr. Ripley came in about that time, and then Jack Eidson got here. Smith and Whalen were brothers-in-law.

And then Dr. Leo Roan had his office up there in what we called the old J.B. Alvis home, a big old brick home up there where Goodyear is now. And that's where Dr. Leo Roan had his office. Dr. Leo Roan was before his brother, Dr. John L. Roan, who is still in town.

J.B. Alvis was a cotton buyer and a watermelon buyer and all this and that. But those were the old-timers.

Dr. Russell probably delivered morc babies than any other doctor ever in Parker County. The doctors drove many miles until it got to where you bring them to town and go to the hospital. But Dr. Russell would go to the country, wherever they might be, Springtown, Dennis, wherever. He'd go out and deliver babies and probably delivered more babies than any other doctor in town.

Dr. Russell and Allen and Funk started what was the Medical and Surgical Clinic, the little hospital we had over there on the corner of Waco and Columbia where the Central Taxing Authority is now. They are the ones who started out. And then of course, Dr. Joe Nelson came in.

Then Dr. Brogdon came in. But I may have missed one or two who've been there since.

But the old-timers, Chandler and McKenzie and MacNelly and Campbell. They were the ones originally here. And I think there was a Dr. Ripley long before my time.

Dr. MacNelly, back in the bootleg days, they made whiskey

and bottled it in half-gallon fruit jars, and it was clear. Now Joe Gilbert was sheriff. Well, Dr. MacNelly, he liked a little toddy occasionally, so he was one first Monday – I think it was a First Monday, or a Saturday. Anyway, he was out of whiskey and his bootlegger had come to town in his wagon and team, so Dr. MacNelly went over there and got him a half-gallon of whiskey.

As he carried it along, he didn't have it in a paper sack or anything. Now as he was walking back to his office, he ran into the sheriff, and the sheriff said, "Doctor, what have you got in your hand there?"

He said, "Whiskey," and just kept walking.

1856 Log Cabin- Parker Co.

Early lawyers, law and public servants

I started out with Frank Fulgham and our law firm went by the name of Fulgham and Borden. After Frank left, Roy Joe Grogan came in, and it was Borden and Grogan. Then in 1955, I.B. Hand came in and it was Borden and Hand. Later we took in Austin Zellers, and it was Borden, Hand and Zellers. After John Westoff got out of law school, it was Borden, Hand, Zellers and Westoff. Today it is just Borden and Westoff in our new building on Santa Fe Drive.

When I got out of law school in 1936, there were not many lawyers. In thinking back, there was Grindstaff, Zellers and Hutchinson up over the Citizens Bank and V.P. Craven had an office up there also. I think Mr. Shadle had died by that time, but before his death it was Hood and Shadle in the Kuteman Building. Nolan Queen officed up there in the same building. Next, I think of Preston Martin and his son-in-law Ben Hagman on the southeast corner of the square up over the gas company. Then we had old Judge Temple, I think his initials were J.F. And then I remember the McCalls, H.C. Shropshire and Ward Bankhead, who officed over the First National Bank. And of course Judge Carter was the judge. I can't think of any other lawyers when I came back in 1939.

All the rest of the lawyers, like Frank Fulgham, went to law school for one year and took the bar examination. Or like V.P. Craven and Hutch Hutchinson, they studied at home. Hutch was the county clerk and V.P. was the county superintendent and they studied law while they were in office, and then took the bar exam. Most lawyers did this in the old days.

Also, back in the old days, you had maybe two or three lawyers who were judges out of Fort Worth, and they came over and gave you an oral exam and that was it. My law class was the last one that didn't have to take the bar examination. Now when you graduate from law school, there's a long test and it takes a couple or three days to answer all the questions.

Now, you know, back in the old days, most of the public offices in the courthouse were on a fee basis – you did not actually draw a salary. You got a certain fee for whatever you did. Now, when I was prosecuting attorney, the limit for my salary was $3,000. The first year I exceeded, or you might say, I took in more fees than the $3,000. But I was only allowed to keep $3,000. If I didn't take in the $3,000, I just got whatever I took in.

Everybody but the Commissioners Court was on the "fee system." The District Judge and the County Judge also got paid on the fee system. Whatever you brought in, you got that amount up to a certain limit, and then you couldn't get any more.

I had a secretary, but I had to pay her out of my money, and that was one of the expenses of the office. So we didn't get rich very quickly. But we didn't have a lot of taxes then either.

I sometimes get amused when we've got a county attorney and a district attorney and each one of them has two or three assistants and three or four investigators, and they draw $100,000 or more or something like that. Times have changed.

SIX OF ONE, A DOZEN OF THE OTHER

In those days, for any felony, you had to have a 12-man jury. Any misdemeanor, you had a six-man jury. Now, the county court and the justice court had six-man juries only.

The district court always had a 12-man jury. They didn't try any criminal cases in the district court except felony cases.

When I was district attorney, I tried all of them. I tried everything from the justice of the peace cases to the district court cases.

Bill Bledsoe

Bill – the man that Bill shot was a stranger through here. Bill killed him right over in the northwest corner of the square. And I was the prosecuting attorney. And Bill – he said, "Oh, there's nothing to it. It was self-defense," and this and that.

And I said, "No, we're going to present it to the grand jury, Bill."

And I said, "Limitation never runs out on a murder. So let's present it to the grand jury and let them no bill you, and this will be the last of it."

So that's what we did. Bill was a good man.

He had a daughter, Dorothy, and a son, Bill Jr. One of his son-in-laws used to sell hog meat, sausage, and all that. He was a big, tall fellow. When old Bill died, Bill Jr. was with the FFA — the airplane people in Grants, New Mexico. That's where he was.

And I had to call old John Good up here at the Texas Bank – he came from Grants – to see if he knew Bill Jr., but he didn't. I spent a couple of nights in Grants, and I just wondered whatever happened to young Bill Bledsoe. Dorothy's daughter, Jeanie Vowel, married Sam Fox, son of Lige Fox, who worked for the health department here. Sam had a brother, Jim Fox.

Parker County Constable for 17 years, from 1943 to 1956.

THE SLEEPING HIGHWAY PATROLMAN

We had one highway patrolman that was prone to go to sleep riding in the vehicle – or anything. And they rode motorcycles a lot then. And, see, this was about 1939 or '40. And this fellow – Mullindorf was his name. He would go to sleep riding that motorcycle, and he couldn't drive. So, he rode with others. A lot of times, they rode, you know – two of them together on patrol.

WOLF IN THE NIGHT

You know, I knew one of those old-time Texas Rangers, old Lone Wolf Gonzales, they called him. He was an old-timer. I mean – a good one. In fact, he spent the night at our house.

I was the prosecuting attorney, and he was up here on something on a case. And I talked to him, said, "Where are you going to stay the night?"

"Well," he said, "Ross Robertson said I could have a bed up there in the jail."

And I said, "No, you ain't going to sleep up there."

I said, "Why don't you come home and spend the night with us."

So I knew those stories about Lone Wolf Gonzales – that's what they called him. He wore two six-shooters, the old-time six-shooters. I remember Texas Rangers Bob Crowder, Ernest Daniel, Levi Duncan, Lone Wolf Gonzales, E.J. Wimberly and Jay Banks.

WHISKEY ALLEY

When I was DA, I suggested to the Commissioners Court, that, hey, "All those guys selling liquor are laying up there in that jail. Why don't we just get a chain gang and let them work a little, as long as we're feeding them and all?"

So they agreed to it. The city joined in with us, and we had Uncle Dick Doggett (he was an old police officer) to guard them. And Slats Linton was one of those filed on. But Slats always had the money to pay his fine.

So they were working on that street down there. They were working Whiskey Alley down by the Kemp Wagonyard. They had the two-by-sixes, top rails on that thing. Old Slats goes up and gets him a big, long cigar, and he climbs up on that top rail right above where they were working, lit that old cigar and leaned back, and said, "Yeah, you durn criminals, you don't think us taxpayers are gonna just let you lay up there in that jail and eat that good food without working for it. This is good for you."

He kept on, until finally Uncle Dick said, "Slats, if you don't shut up, I'm gonna put you in there with them."

TRIALS AND BOOTLEGGERS

Oh, Lord, you know there wasn't much amusing that went on in trials. Some little something would come up, but the trials that we tried were really real serious.

I never did try any moonshiners. When I got out of school, liquor over the rest of the state was legal. Parker County was dry. It was a dry area. But I don't think I ever – well, making whiskey, bootleg whiskey, I never did try a case. But, yeah, I did try a case of transporting. The stills were busted at that time and put on the courthouse lawn for everyone to see.

The Wild Cat Liquor Still on old Smith Farm, 6 miles southeast of Weatherford. V.P. Craven prosecuted the case as county attorney.

C.N. Sullivan- country attorney, Tom Gray- deputy sheriff, Barney Barker- deputy sheriff, C.B. Cato- constable

Famous Jury Trial

Attorneys and court officials for the R.H. Hamilton trial in Weatherford, Texas – District Court fall term, 1929. The verdict was Not Guilty.
Front: Edward W. Thomerson, district attorney, Amarillo; Hugh H. Cooper, special state attorney, Amarillo; Hon. J.E. Carter, judge, 43rd District Court, Weatherford; Simpson, defense, Amarillo; F.O. McKinsey, defense, Weatherford; Robert Underwood Sr., defense, Amarillo; Eloy Fletcher, defense, Amarillo.
Back: Grady Hazlewood, assistant district attorney, Amarillo; Sam J. Little, court reporter, Weatherford; E.H. Grindstaff, state attorney, Weatherford; V.P. Craven, county attorney, Parker County, state; Sam Shadle, defense, Weatherford; C.B. Reeder, defense, Amarillo; R.B. Hood, defense, Weatherford; Bob Underwood Jr., defense, Amarillo.

JACK BORDEN
Weatherford Parade
1948 or 1949

Jack Borden still rides in the rodeo parades in Weatherford. However, instead of riding one horse, he rides 300 horses, along with Boley Pearson and Dub Jordan. The sign on the side of the 300 horses reads: "Posse members for more than 50 years."

PARKER COUNTY SHERIFF'S POSSE

I'm the only living charter member of the Sheriff's Posse. I got in in 1947. The group that really organized it, there were 12 or 14 of them. Red Wood was one, and he was the one that got me to join. And J.Y. Crum.

Red called me one day, and he said, "Hey, we're organizing a sheriff's posse, and we need a lawyer, and we need four more members." And said, "I'll come by and pick you up."

I lived in those apartments right up there on the corner of Spring and Lamar. And I said, "Red, it's just a block. I'll walk down there."

So I got down there, and I became a member that night, and then I got the charter going. This was in January 1947.

We met in the old Roger Williams Garment Factory on the north side of Palo Pinto Street. This is the same building where Remembrance Flower Shop is now.

I was asked to help write the by-laws. Funny thing was, none of us knew anything about by-laws of that nature. Tom Saunders said his wife was a member of the Women's Junior League in Fort Worth and that they had by-laws, so I asked him to bring me a sct of theirs, and we'd discuss them. We actually wrote ours with some similarity.

Jack Borden, Weldon Jordan, Gene Polser, Boley Pearson

CHARTER MEMBERS

Parker county sheriff's posse
The original 13 were

J.Y. Crum	Dave Hudson	Tom B. Saunders
Fletcher Dalton	Forest Lindsay	Roger Williams
Marsh Farmer	Frank McEntire	L.T. "Red" Wood
Walker Good	Cullen Robinson	
Aaron Hays	Loyd Smith	

The next seven were

Jack Borden	Ferd Slocum	H.K. Whaley
Walter Caraway	Ray Smyth	S.A. Wheeler
Barney Phillips		

Making 20 Charter Members

Sheriffs since posse was organized

John Young	Coy Carter	Ben Whiteman
Louis Peoples	Billy Cain	Jay Brown

Some older Sheriffs of Parker County who never heard of this kind of "Posse."

Row 1: S.S. Gilbert, 1910; John R. Brown, 1918
Row 2: Joe Gilbert, 1922; Barney R. Barker, 1930

CAPTIANS 1947-2003

1947 – Aaron Hays
1948 – Tom B. Saunders III
1949 – Ferd Slocum
1950 – Walter Caraway
1951 – H.K. Whaley
1952 – Morris Sands
1953 – H. Calhoun
1954 – Loyd Hinkle
1955 – Ray Pafford
1956 – Ray Smyth
1957 – Couts Holland
1958 – Floyd Tinsley Jr.
1959 – Acme Shaw
1960 – L.D. "Bill" Murray
1961 – Boley Pearson
1962 – Charles Merritt
1963 – Weldon Jordan
1964 – Eugene Polser
1965 – Edgar Bowden
1966 – Henry Maddux
1967 – Forrest G. Reid
1968 – Sammie Skiles
1969 – Dr. John T. Brackeen Jr.
1970 – L.S. Young
1971 – Walter Worthington
1972 – Jimmy Hemphill
1973 – W.R. Riddle Jr.
1974 – Bill Jordon
1975 – D.C. "Dude" Woodruff
1976 – M.C. Thomas
1977 – Don Woodruff
1978 – Martin Brown
1979 – Thomas Riddle
1980 – Coy Carter
1981 – Holton Riddle
1982 – Kenneth Hamilton
1983 – Perry Mader
1984 – Jerry Durant
1985 – Mike Thomas
1986 – Leroy Schoonover
1987 – Rick Merritt
1988 – Dr. Noel Bryan
1989 – Herbert Fowler
1990 – Herman Woodard
1991 – Bob Elder
1992 – Harold Swain
1993 – Bill Veselka
1994 – Earl Fletcher
1995 – Mack Young
1996 – Avery (Butch) Morris
1997 – Fred Thomas
1998 – Jack Parker
1999 – Wayne Bryant
2000 – Duane Bailey
2001 – Arlie Ashley
2002 – Mark Riebe
2003 – Judd Jordan

CURRENT POSSE MEMBERS

Jim Addison
Jack Alexander
Calvin Allen
Arlie Ashley
Josh Ashley
Ronnie Ashley
Duane Bailey
Dale Ballard
Robbie Ballard
James T. Barnett
Clarence Beavers
J.P. Binion
Mark S. Binion
Jerry Blaisdell
Billy Blue
Jack Borden
Jim Bradford
Jay Brown
Martin R. Brown
Noel Bryan
Wayne Bryant
Coy Carter
Guy Carter
Clay Cowdrey
Maurice Curfman
Melvin Dale
Fred Davies
Roy Glen Densmore
R.L. Dugan
Jim Duncan
Jerry Durant
Bob Elder
Lewis Wayne Ellis
Joe Ernst
Travis Faulkner
J.W. Ford
Jeff Ford
Rick Ford
Herb Fowler
Jamie French
Tim French
Tommy French
Don Gill
Bob Glenn
Gary Grote
C.A. Guess
Rusty Hale
Jay Hall
Kenneth Hamilton
Kevin Hamilton
Pat Hamilton
Shane Harris
James L. Hemphill
Justin High
Dennis Hooks
Doyle Hutcheson
Jamie Jennings
Charlie Johnson
Joe Dean Johnson
Stoney Johnson
Terry Johnson
Bill Jordan
Judd Jordan
Weldon Jordan
Kerry Kelley
Monty Kemp
W.P. Koonce
Thomas Lackey
Bob Lambert
Tony Lavite
Phil Livingston
Henry Maddux
Jimmy R. Maddux
Perry Mader
Mel Mallory
Kirk Martin
Jeff Mauldin
Ron Mayberry

Bill McDavid
David McDavid
Roland McWhorter
Rick Merritt
David Milhollon
Tom B. Mills
Charles Beggs Moncrief
Avery Morris
Robert D. Muir
R.D. Myers III
David Nash
Sam W. Nash
Tommy H. Newberry
Buddy Newsome
Francis Nichols
Randy O'Neal
Jack Parker
Bill Parkey
Benny Peacock
Blaine Peacock
Craig Peacock
Boley Pearson
Larry Peck
Bill Pedigo
R.G. Bob Perkins
Robert E. Phillips
Thomas E. Riddle
Tim Riddle
W. Holton Riddle
William E. Riddle
W.R. Riddle Jr.
Mark Riebe
John Robinson
David N. Rockwell
David Rogers
Joe Ross
David Rothrock
Ernie Rutledge
Bobby Sandlin
T.B. Saunders IV
Leroy Schoonover
Stephen Schult
Jimmy Sharp
Justin Shifflett
L.R. Sullivan
Larry Sullivan
Roy Sutherland
Harold Swain
Bob Tallman
Fred Thomas
J.G. Buck Thomas
Marvin Thomas
Mike Thomas
Tommy Thomas
Willard Thomas
Cody Todd
R.D. Todd
Bill Vanhoosier
Bill Veselka
John Westhoff
Charles E. Wetherell
Roger Williams
Richard F. Williamson
Gene Wood
Herman Woodard
D.C. Woodruff
Don Woodruff
Brookes Worthington
Walter Worthington
Cleatus Wright
Derrell Young
James Young
Mack Young
Jim Zacharias

HONEST JOHN

Honest John, he was running for office. He drove over to Azle and he'd put out a story, a wild story, and there wasn't any truth in it. He'd put it out over there, and then he'd go to Dennis and tell a different story. Well, by the time they found the truth out of this one over here, why, he'd already got this one in Dennis spreading around. And he just did that everywhere. He enjoyed doing that. Honest John, we called him. He was a character.

I think we first – the Sheriff's Posse – the first parade we rode in was the stock show parade.

You know, the sheriff is an honorary member of the Sheriff's Posse. And he said, "OK, you boys. Now I'm going to be sitting at that county line over there, and I'm going to stop every one of you. And if you've got liquor on your breath, you're going to the jail house."

And some of them went on the old highway. They turned by Aledo. And of course, he was just kidding. He didn't do it.

Herb Fowler advertises the Parker County Sheriff's Posse rodeo where'er he can.

TALES OF THE PAST WITH JACK

Round Ice Co.

When I was in my first year in Weatherford College, a gentleman by the name of Lee – and I've forgotten what Mr. Lee's initials were, but he built an ice plant on South Main Street just off the square right behind what we used to call the old Woodhouse building. It was right across the street to the east of where Dr. Campbell's old office was, right across on South Main.

And he called it the Round Ice Company. That was the name of it. Mr. Lee had come up with the theory of making ice in round cubes, and it was harder and didn't melt as fast as the block ice. Well, we found out later that round ice didn't fit very well in the square refrigerator, so he started making block ice as well and used that round ice for other things.

Mr. Lee was looking for somebody to deliver ice. So he went to Coach Beard down at Weatherford College, and I was one of the ones that Coach Beard recommended. I went up there and talked to the old gentleman, and he said, "I'm going to hire you."

He said, "I got two pairs of mules and two wagons down at the wagon yard, and I want you to go down there and harness up a pair of those mules, hook 'em to one of those wagons, and drive around the square. I just want you to drive around the square."

Well, I got down there, and old Cat Medford was sort of the keeper of the animals down there. (Once, he had found a hole, and he didn't know what was in it, so he just went in with his hands, and there was a bobcat in there. And that's where he got the name Cat Medford.)

And there were four or five loafers hanging around. I told Cat what I wanted, and he says, "OK. There's two – there's a couple – there's a pair of brown mules and a pair of red mules."

Well, I knew enough about mules that I took the brown ones.

Of course, those old boys got to looking at them, and me. You know, I had a white shirt on and all, and they got to snickering about that old city boy trying to get the harness on those mules and that I'd put it on backwards, and everything else.

Now Old Cat knew who I was. And he said, "Well, now. I'll tell you, if y'all think that's funny and you're going to bet your money, I'll just cover your bets."

Well, I don't know whether they bet a dime apiece or a quarter; either one would have been a whole lot of money back in 1929. So old Cat, he just covered all the bets.

Well, I got my mules out, and I went over and got a bridle, and the first one didn't want to take the bit. So I got down under the jaw, you know, and squeezed under the neck and mouth against his teeth, and that mule opened his mouth. Those other guys – I thought they were going to hang old Cat.

They said, "You knew who that guy was."

But yeah, I drove those mules around the square. In fact, I delivered ice there until the summer before my senior year in law school. The sign on the wagon said Round Ice Company, and those wagons were covered. We just carried the round ice with regular ice tongs. The back end of the wagon was open, and you'd slide your ice in there, and then you'd keep it covered with a tarp. And as you used up a block, you'd pull another one out and cover it back up with a tarp.

I never will forget the Ruckers, Oscar and Clarence. The Ruckers drove wagons, also. Anyhow, my mules and I stopped up on Spring Street, and I guess I was sparking some young gal up there and stayed in the house longer than I should have. When I came out, my mules were gone. So I started walking, and I found them down there on Spring Street just before you get to York Avenue. The Ruckers had stopped them.

So I got in, turned them around, and Mr. Rucker said, "Now, Jack, do you want to teach them not to walk off and leave you anymore?"

I said, "I sure do."

He had a little long, leather black snake, and he handed it to me.

He said, "OK. You've got them turned around. Now, you start them, and you just bathe them with this black snake from their ears to their rear ends from here to where they started."

And he said, "I'll guarantee you when you turn around and say, 'Whoa,' they're going to stop and they're not going to walk off."

I did that, and they never walked off and left me anymore.

We had to get the mules at the wagon yard each day, but the wagons were at the ice plant. You know, you had that old leather thing on your back to keep the ice from dripping down. Well, it was open at each end, and after you'd carried ice in the summertime for an hour or two, well, it got water-soaked and you'd go in and there'd be a little trickle of water following you out and in. So I got me a big old bath towel, and when I went out, I'd mop that water up.

Well, it didn't take that long to get around, and I had more ice business than I could take care of. What hurt the block ice people was that I was quite a salesman.

Mrs. J.B. Alvis up there, I delivered ice to her. And every other day, nearly, there would be a plate of cookies up there for me.

I picked up more dogs and cats on the route and dropped them some other place. I dropped one at W.D. Newberry's. Mrs. Newberry – Mary – I went to school to her when I was coming to town to go to school occasionally. And I brought them a German shepherd puppy and left it for Ann and Bill. They were just little kids. And the next day, Mary worked on me just like she did when she was a schoolteacher. "You take this dog away from here, Jack Borden, and don't you ever bring anything up here. If I want anything, I'll let you know."

I delivered that ice until my last year in law school. I had one course that I had to do something on, so I stayed down there the whole summer instead of coming home and working. But I worked at that ice plant. I started out with them, and I worked every summer that I was here.

Ben K. Green's father operated the ice plant that was over there just across the viaduct. That was Texas Power and Light Company, TP&L. See, the old man Green there, and then Hugh, I think, was the one that stayed with the ice plant.

ROUND ICE CO.

We are manufacturers of
Ice only
Pure, Sparkling Ice
Prompt service

Phone 712 S. Main St.

Weatherford, Texas

MR. AKARD- MAKING THE RULES

Old Mr. Akard lived up on Palo Pinto Street, and he lived up there forever. And he would go home, drive home in the afternoon, and he'd be going out west and he was going to the south side of Palo Pinto, so he'd just cut across as anybody else would.

Well, one day a fellow came along from Mineral Wells and hit him and got out. And they got to looking at the damage, and so this man said, "Well, why, Mr. Akard, did you cross there?"

He said, "I've been turning across this way now for the last 40 years, and everybody knows that I cross here, and it was your fault that you ran into me."

ED BOWDEN- PE(S)T

Mary Hunter Newberry taught school at Second Ward, and I went to school at Second Ward.

Ed Bowden and I, they had one seat at the front that had one desk and would seat two people. It was a wide seat. Ed and I shared that. We sat up there.

We were supposed to be the teacher's pets or – I don't know whether it was the pets, or pests. Maybe we were pests.

OBIE BEENE AND THE OLD MAN CLASS

Our Sunday school class at First Baptist Church is also known as the old man class, or the fellowship class. My friend Obie Beene and I are members of that class. And a few years ago, we had a lesson on adultery, and the teacher taught the lesson about regular adultery and about lust, and after all that, he said, "Now, if you see a good-looking young gal walking down the street with a short skirt on, is it a sin to look?"

And our class kicked that around a while and finally the teacher said, "Obie, how old do you get before you stop looking?"

There was no hesitation on Obie's part. He just came right out and said, "I don't know – I'm just 98."

BOB BRAZELTON, SMOOTH TALKER

I knew Uncle Bob Brazelton, as everybody called him. He had a mule barn down on Whiskey Alley. He had a man in there one day looking for a mule. He had a nice-looking young mule there, so this old boy looked it over. He said, "Well, Bob, get him out and let's see him walk across this corral here." Bob slapped the old mule on the rear, and he starts hopping off and ran right into a fence. The old man says, "Now, Bob, is that mule blind?" He says, "No, he just don't give a damn." Another story on Uncle Bob was that he lived over on the north side of town and he had an automobile that he wanted to sell. Being a horse trader, he knew how to sell it. The man asked him, "Now, who has driven this car?" "Nobody except me." "Well, Uncle Bob, where have you driven this?" He said, "I live on the north side of town. I just drive it to work and back, downhill both ways."

ANDY BRINKLEY, PANCAKE MAN

I may have told you before – while I was in Weatherford College, I started hauling ice for the old Round Ice Company on South Main Street. At that time, Andy Brinkley operated the café over on the east side of the square, south of Fort Worth Street. And I'd go in there and eat breakfast. And Andy made the best flapjacks, hotcakes, that anybody ever tasted.

I asked him one day, "Mr. Brinkley, how do you keep them from sticking?" He said, "Jack, when you get your pan hot, you just get you an Irish potato, cut it half in two, and just rub it around that pan," and said, "They won't ever stick."

I cooked them for years, and just like he said – no sticking. I told my dad how to do it, and he cooked them.

Oh, I knew Andy Brinkley. He had those handlebar mustaches. Yeah. He was one of my best friends. Peter's Café was later where Andy Brinkley was. It became Peter's Café.

GRANNY BYRON

That's when Granny Byron was principal up there at 2nd Ward. Mrs. Byron lived out there northeast on the hill. They called her Granny Byron; her name was Ashley.

Well, her room was upstairs over on the northwest corner. And the older children were in – I guess I must have been 12, 14 years old, before they went to high school. And Mrs. Byron would – now, she wasn't reserved. If she wanted some boy, she'd go in the boy's restroom to get him out. She just walked and got him by the ear and pulled him out of there.

Well, the story is that one time she said, "OK, I've got to be gone a little bit." So she goes outside, and there's a big, old oak tree growing nearby, and she climbed that oak tree and peeped in the window to see if everybody was behaving.

She also made grown boys sit on her lap in front of the entire room for misbehaving. ???? embarrassing. I was able to avoid that.

COY CARTER

I knew Coy Carter. I knew the sheriff here. In fact, his dad died young. I had known that family ever since I can remember. After the war, we were going somewhere and we stopped for breakfast early one morning about 7 o'clock at a Holiday Inn on the turnpike between Fort Worth and Dallas. And we'd just gotten out of the car and we saw Coy Carter.

And I said, "Carter, what are you doing at this hotel, coming out at this time of the morning?" And I said, "Your wife, is she with you? If not, I guess I'll have to go home and call her and tell her where I found you."

He said, "Jack, wait a minute, wait a minute. I've got a prisoner. We just stopped here, like you, to get breakfast. Don't start telling my wife any tales."

JUDGE J.E. CARTER

Judge J.E. Carter was trying a case. The jury was there, and in those days, when they came in they'd all be sworn, and then the judge would say, "OK, now if any of you have any excuses, why, you may get up and give them to me, and if I think it's a good enough excuse that you can't serve on the jury, why, I'll let you go."

There were four or five or six people that stood up and gave various reasons. Well, the last one was standing and the judge says, "OK, what's your problem?"

Well, he said, "Judge, my wife and I have only been married about nine months." And he said, "She is pregnant, and we're expecting the child any time." And said, "Since it's our first child, I'd like to be there when it happens."

And the judge said, "Well, I think that's a pretty good reason. I'm going to excuse you." Then a young fellow popped up. The judge said, "Oh, do you have an excuse?" And he said, "Yes, sir." The judge said, "OK, what is it?" "Well, Judge, my wife and I have only been married about two weeks, and I'm expecting her to get pregnant, and I want to be there when it happens." But the judge did not tell him to leave.

J.E. Carter moved to Texas in 1890. He served the county as judge of the 43rd District Court from 1929 to 1951.

V.P. CRAVEN- A WORTHY OPPONENT

V.P. was – he didn't have all the finesse and whatnot like R.B. Hood did, but he had a way about him. He knew all of the jurors. See, he was a schoolteacher here, and he could count on his schoolchildren coming along for jury duty. And everybody thought V.P Craven was the greatest thing that ever lived. I lost two or three criminal cases in the entire time that I was prosecuting, and the only ones I lost were to Craven.

I had one case where Grindstaff, Zellers, and Hutchson and R.B. Hood were all on the same side – on the other side of me –and I got a conviction. But Mr. Craven, he'd get up there and he'd raise his voice, you know, and the first thing you know, he'd convince some of these jurors that hey, this is – this is so-and-so.

It seemed he took the underdogs. He took the position, "Well, I'm just an old, poor, country boy, and I'm going to take care of all these old, poor country boys."

V.P. CRAVEN AT SPRINGTOWN

V.P. Craven, a former prosecutor here in Parker County, had a case out of Springtown where one man was accused of kicking another man in the seat of the pants all the way across the Springtown square. And a lot of people saw it, so they went out and filed and they got a jury of six good men out of Springtown. They tried it, and these witnesses all came in and testified, "Yeah, I saw old John Doe kick old Joe Blow's rear end all the way across the square." They did all the testimony and the jury went out and found old John Doe not guilty. Mr. Craven told them, he said, "Well, when I get back to the office, I'm going to write the legislature and tell them the assault statue on the books does not apply when old John Doe kicks Joe Blow's rear end across the square in Springtown." The two men involved were fairly well-known citizens of Springtown. This was around 1930 to 1934. Maybe some old-timers at Springtown will remember this.

V.P. Craven County Attorney 1929

THE POCKETKNIFE AND ED DILL

Well, I've known Ed Dill since I was a kid, ever since I can remember anybody. He lived up the creek from us. And he only had one child, a daughter, Winnie. And in those days, your hardware company or store carried your bill until you gathered your crops. Then you went in and paid it off, and they'd always give you a pocketknife or something. Well, Mr. Ed gave me a pocketknife, and I was, oh, 6, 7, 8 years old, I guess, when he gave me my first pocketknife. Well, I'd lose them. Every time I'd get one, I'd lose it.

Well, we were off to Arizona and got back here in '29, and they had their homecoming, or reunion, out at Clear Fork Baptist Church out at Dicey. And we went out there, and Mr. Dill was there.

So, we were sitting around talking, and he said, "Jack, let me see your pocketknife." I said, "Mr. Ed, I don't have a pocketknife." "Well," he said, "I'm going to give you one, and this is the last one I'm going to give you."

Now, this was in September 1929, and he pulled a pearl-handled pocketknife out and gave it to me. And I've been carrying it daily. I've been carrying that daily since September 1929.

The only time I ever used my badge wrongfully in the FBI – in those days, your pants had a pocket, what we call a watch pocket, and that's where I always carried the knife. In the FBI, when you started out in the morning, you always slapped to see if you had your badge, and you slapped to see if you had your credentials. And your gun, you always slapped to see if you had it. I had a fourth place, that knife.

Well, I took some pants to the cleaners one morning, and I took off, and I got about seven or eight miles out of town. That's when I was living in Tallahassee. I slapped my gun, my badge, my credentials, and I slapped – Oh Lord, I didn't have the pocketknife.

So I wheeled that government car around in the middle of

the highway, and I went back to the cleaners. And when I got back, I told the man, "I left some slacks here awhile ago, and I just wondered if you found a pocketknife in the watch pocket."

"Well, he said. "I never looked at it." But he said, "The black man back there, he does that." So I went back and asked him.

"No sir, I didn't see anything." Well, I just pulled that gold badge out and sort of shoved my coat back where he could see that six-shooter, and I said, "I came after that pearl-handled pocketknife." And he said, "Yes sir." And he pulled it out and handed it to me.

Jack Borden and his pocketknife 2003

MRS. GILBERT'S BROKEN ARM

Mrs. Gilbert broke her arm. She was up on a stool or something at the kitchen cabinet and broke an arm. And Irby, her daughter, called me and said, "Mother's in the hospital, Jack." And I said, "What's wrong?" She said, "She broke her arm." And I said, "What happened?" "Well," she said, "She wanted something high up in the kitchen cabinet, and she got on her chair to get up there and she fell." And I said, "OK, I'll be over and see her." So I went over, and I walked to the door. And I said, "Mrs. Gilbert, let me give you a little bit of advice." And she said, "What is it, Jack?" I said, "Why don't you put that liquor bottle that you were drinking out of on a lower shelf where you won't have a problem." She said, "I'm going to kill you."

WELL-DRESSED WALKER GOOD

Walker Good was telling me one time that he came down here as foreman for Saunders Ranch, and he had three or four more horses than he could keep out there of his own. So he decided to sell them. He took them down to Dee Jenkins. That's when Dee had his automobile agency on the corner of Elm and Fort Worth Street. He and Dee haggled and haggled and finally agreed on a price of $94 for all three of the horses.

When they got through, Dee said, "Take them on down to that little pasture on the creek and turn them loose and come back by and I'll pay you."

Well, Walker was just an old cowhand, and he wore Levis and if his shirt had a little tear in it, that didn't bother him. Instead of a belt, he wore what was called a pigging string, which was a little piece of short rope that he tied around his waist instead of a belt. He came back and Dee gave him a hundred dollar bill, and Walker looked at it and said, "Mr. Jenkins, I don't have change for a hundred dollar bill."

Dee looked him up and down, and said, "Well, no more money than you spend on clothes, you ought to have it."

ROY GROGAN

Roy – when Roy got out of law school, why, we were still in – well, it was originally the Korean conflict we were getting into. He thought that he would go into the Navy. He came up to the office and visited with me, and I said, "Roy, let me tell you what to do. Make an application and get into the FBI. Once you get in the FBI, you will be set for life."

So he got in the FBI and stayed a year or two, and then he got out. He came in my office and officed with me until he ran for district attorney. We were partners. This was after I got out of the FBI and Frank was the district judge then. And I was over there by myself. So Roy came in with me and stayed there until he ran and was elected DA. He stayed with me a year or two. I guess he succeeded I.B. in the district attorney's office.

Roy Joe Grogan, District Attorney
Parker County 1955-1959
Jack's law partner

YOUNG JIM SHAW

We're talking about Young Jim, because Old Jim, son of T.J. Shaw, married Kate Abbott, and he died and she never remarried. This is her son, Jim. Married a Millburn.

Jim got to be deputy sheriff. Lester Stewart needed a deputy, so he selected Jim as a deputy. Bill Bledsoe had an old six-shooter. One of his relatives and a man by the name of Foreman met on what is now Farmer Road. They were gunning for each other, and they both pulled guns and each one of them was killed. Bill had his ancestor's gun. And it was about, looked like it was 12 inches long. Well, Jim was a short fellow, about 5'7" or 8". When Jim came to be sworn in, we had it all fixed up. We had a belt with a holster and said, "OK, Jim, we'll put your gun on." We swung that six-shooter on old Jim, and I'll tell you, the barrel reached down to his knees and the butt of it was up under his arm. Later on then, he ran for and was elected county tax assessor/collector.

Jim and I were real good friends. And we'd go fishing occasionally; we went fishing somewhere out in the east part of Parker County. He broke down and told me that he had cancer.

Afterwards, he came up to my office in the courthouse. He was down on the ground floor in the southeast corner and I was on the second floor in the northeast corner. This is when he told me the details of the cancer. He said, "Pull you up a chair."

I will never forget, we had two chairs, and we sat down with our feet up on the sill and he told me about it and told me what he wanted me to do. I don't think I've ever seen a braver man in all my life. He sat there, and said, "Now, Jack, I'm going to die. I just got in this office, and I haven't even served my term and I would like for my wife to finish my term."

I told him, "Jim, if that's the only thing bothering you before you die, you just rest assured that that will happen."

That very day, I got in touch with Peck Nichols, who was one of the commissioners. I believe Tom Ervin was the county judge. Maybe Sam Nash was the commissioner of Precinct 3. I've forgotten who the other commissioners were. Anyhow, I got them together and I told them the story, and they said, "You tell Jim not to worry, that we will appoint his wife to succeed him." And they did. And later on, she ran and was elected a time or two. I think Bill Carr succeeded her.

We used to go down to Spring Creek to have lunch with Jim's mother, "Mother Kate." Me, the sheriff, Ross Robertson, maybe Jake Long and the other guys. There'd be maybe four or five of us. And Miss Kate, as I called her, she'd fix lunch for all of us. We'd just have a big time sitting there eating.

They tell a story on me, I don't know whether it's the truth or not, but the story was told on me that they asked me to return thanks, and I said, "Oh Lord, Oh God, aw, hell Jim, I can't do it. You do it!"

JOHN TURNER'S WAY WITH WORDS

John Turner was the constable and later was sheriff. They lived out there close to us where I grew up, east of town. He and his wife and the children. The children were all born out there. There was one of them married to a Wilkes Burkhalter. And one of them was the tall, tall blond-headed guy. Oh, Lord, he was a nice kid. I think he went in the service.

Now, I won't forget when John was sheriff because I've known him forever, since I was a kid. When he was a sheriff and I was district attorney, why, he came up to my office one day. And we'd had a rape case reported. And so John and I were talking, and he said, "Jack," he said. "I think it's the rape-ee." And I said, "Rape-ee?" And he said, "Yeah." And I said, "Well, what in the world is rape-ee?" He said, "That's where the woman is willing."

The county attorney and the district attorney was all the same at that time.

DISTRICT CLERK KEEPS DRINK IN SAFE

Homer Turpin was the district clerk. At that time, he was in the southwest corner [of the courthouse] on the ground floor. If I'm not mistaken, there were iron doors and originally, that was made for the district clerk's office. Like in the county clerk's office, they have steel doors, and steel shutters for the windows so that you can lock it up. Well, there was a safe in there that he kept all the records in.

And Homer had lost a leg when he was a young man, and he would tell me that the leg would just hurt all the time. Others had told me that when they lost a limb that it aches and itches and all. He was in a whole lot of pain. Well, around 5 p.m., around closing-up time, Homer kept him a bottle, and he'd go into the safe and take a drink. When he did, why he would [whistling sound]. And the sheriff's office was next door and we'd be there and hear old Homer whistle and we'd say, "Uh oh, about closing time. Homer's had a little drink." He was taking it for pain.

Left to right: Herman Turpin, Goerge Kelly, Bobby Turpin, Mary Ann Kelly and Homer L. Turpin. Homer Turpin served as county clerk in Parker County for four years. He also served as district clerk of Parker County for eight years. The year could be 1935 or near that. Homer and Dora (Crow) Turpin raised 3 boys. Homer Jr., Jack (who died at age 19) and Bobby G. Turpin. Place: Grandpa Turpin's home on the southwest corner of Franklin Street and 4th Street.

HERSHEL WHALEY

Now, Hershel Whaley's father was a pastor at First Baptist Church, and Hershel had a cleaning shop and got into the automobile business. Well, a used car dealer bought a car off of Hershel and then gave him a check for it. The check was on the Citizens National Bank.

And Whaley sent it through, just made a deposit, and the check came back. He called the man up and said, "That check you gave me for that car came back." He said, "What bank did I write it on?" "You wrote it on the Citizens."

"I don't know what was the matter with me. We had counter checks and I just picked one up, and see, that's the wrong bank," he said. "Bring it over here and I'll write one on another bank."

So Hershel goes over and the dealer gives him a check on M & F Bank. And Hershel deposited it and it came back. He called the dealer and said, "This check came back." "What bank did I write it on?" "M & F." "Oh, goodness gracious, I've only done business with the First National Bank. I must be losing my mind. Come on over and I'll give you another check."

So he gave him a check on First National and it bounced. So, Hershel went to see him, and this has taken about a week or 10 days and the automobile had already been sold. Hershel said, "Now, sir, I'm tired of these checks. I want my money." And the gentleman said, "Why didn't you say so in the first place?" So he just pulled out the cash and paid. There were some great characters back in that day.

BERNICE WOLFENBERGER'S JOKE

When I was, oh, 14 or 15, I went to the threshing machine and was driving the bundle wagon. Now, in the old days, why they shocked that wheat with your binder, and they tied it, and then they shocked it. Then at the threshing time, why, the bundle wagon would go out and there'd be fellows out there pitching it up to you, and you'd load your bundle wagon and drive it in, and you'd unload it at the threshing machine.

Well, this was my first time in the hay field. And there were three of us, Louis King and then one of those Cabelter boys and I, all our first time. And old Bernice Wolfenberger was there. Now, he was a grown man then.

And one night – we all had army cots that we slept on, those canvas cots. Well, one night – you know how boys were, and my Lord, we'd work and we'd go to bed and go to sleep, and we never knew anything until somebody yelled to get up the next morning. We were threshing on the Vicks' place.

Well, during the night, why, we heard some yelling or something, and all three of us started getting up. And old Bernice had gotten some binder twine, and he'd tied our big toes on each foot to the corner of that cot. So you can imagine how we liked Bernice.

IN THE EYES OF LEE YOUNG

When I was teaching a Bible class at First Baptist Church, Lee Young came one day for a visit. I introduced Lee, and most of the fellows there knew him. I said, "You all know Lee, except there's one thing about him that you don't know, that he has one artificial eye." And it was so perfect that even experts had a hard time, just looking, to determine which is the glass eye.

Not long ago, why, Lee had a man who came in trying to get a loan. Lee was at First National, a loan officer over there. Lee didn't want to make the loan. And the man kept on and Lee said, "I'll tell you what, I have one artificial eye, and if you can tell me which one's artificial, I believe I'll go ahead and make you that loan." The man said, "The Right Eye." Lee said, "How in the world could you tell? I've had experts who couldn't tell. How in the world could you tell it was the artificial eye?" The man said, "It's the only one that had a gleam of sympathy." The man got the loan.

CUB YOUNG

You know, you were asking me about the black people that I've known here. I guess I knew all of them. There was a place called Sand Town that was down there just east of the trades grounds, First Monday grounds.

And Lester Stewart was sheriff, and I was the assistant district attorney. Lester called my office one day, and said, "Hey, I got a report there was a crap game going on down in Sand Town. Would you go down there with Jake Long and me?" And I said sure.

So we got in the car and went down there. We got in the house, and there was four or five or six of those fellows sitting around on the floor with a blanket in front of them; no money, no dice, nothing. But one of them was Cub Young.

So Lester questioned them a little bit, and finally he told them, "I've had a complaint about y'all shooting craps. If I get any more – whether I find any money, any craps or not – I'm going to put y'all in jail."

So we got ready to leave, and Cub said, "Mr. Lester, could I ride to town with y'all?" Lester said, "Sure. Come on." So Cub and I got in the back seat. And Cub said, "I sure was glad y'all come." I said, "Why?" "Well," he said, "I was 65 cents winner, and I was ready to get out of there." I said, "Well, Cub, what did you do with the dice?" He says, "They was just little pee-wee dice, and I just swallowed them."

The first time I saw Cub, I said, "Cub, you passed yet?"

"No sir, I ain't passed yet."

For 25 years, it got to where when he'd see me, he'd say, "Mr. Jack, I ain't passed yet."

He was a character, that Cub was. You know, he was a great baseball pitcher. In this day and time, he'd have gotten the Cy Young award.

CHARLIE AND IKE SIMMONS

There were two brothers, Charlie Simmons and Ike Simmons. Now, Ike was a custodian and shined shoes at the City Barber Shop, and Charlie was at the Palace Barber Shop. Now, Ike was a small fellow. Charlie was a pretty good-sized man. The Palace was over there – the Texas Bank has a part of it now, and the City Barber Shop was on the west side of the square by Corcanges Drug, just right by it. It was next to that building that Vick, Carney and Smith are in now.

Doc Cummins was one of the barbers, and also Jack Dunn. And old Jack, originally he was at the Palace, and then they got together.

But Ike, the story – now I wasn't here when this happened – it happened shortly before I got out of law school. But there was a black preacher who came here and stayed around for a few days and had a little revival back over in Sand Town. Apparently he had been making some overtures – it might have been more than overtures – to another man's wife over there. He came in on the train. Well, when he started to leave, a lot of the black people were at the train. This irate husband shot the guy, shot him twice. But I don't know whether he killed him or not.

But anyhow, Ike was there when it happened. He was at the depot. And they had him on the witness stand to testify. They said, "Now, you were there?" "Yes sir." "Well, how many shots were fired?" "Two." "Well how close together?" Ike clapped his hands twice real fast! And they said, "Well, where were you when the first shot was fired?" "Well, I was standing right there at the depot." "So, where were you when the second shot was fired?" "Well, I was past that blacksmith's shop about 400 feet south." I told present-day Charlie Simmons about that once. He loved it.

MY FRIEND JAKE

There were some amusing things, when I was D.A.. For instance the time Jake Swearingin was fined for lying. What happened is, back in those days, you had to give a little certificate when you sold a car. Jake was in the used car business over there on Whiskey Avenue. And he was supposed to give some little old certificate that cost 25 cents every time he sold a car. That was part of it, sort of like a certificate of title now.

Well, Jake wouldn't give them. And people would come in to me and say, "Jake won't give it, and I can't get it." Then I'd get Jake up there and I had him in three or four times. Jake said, "Jack, it'll never happen again, it'll never happen again.'

It did happen again and I sent for Jake. I said, "Jake you're going to have to pay a fine."

Jake said, "Jack, you wouldn't make me pay a fine for a little old 25 cent thing like that?"

And I said, "No, Jake, I'm not going to make you pay a fine for that. The fact that you don't give a certificate – that doesn't hurt me any." But I said, "You pledged me on your work of honor that this would never happen again." And I said, "Now, it's happened and that hurts me that your broke your word and your promise to me."

He said, "What do you mean?"

And I said, "Well, we're going across the hall to Judge Hawkins' court, and I am going to let him fine you for lying."

So we went over there and, of course, we put out the charge and he was fined. Jake went right from the court over to Tammay Hall, the old Texas Café – bragging that he was the only man in Parker County that had ever been fined for lying.

JOKE PULLED ON BEN HAGMAN

Before I came out of law school, Ben Hagman had been Frank Fulgham's assistant for a time and he had gone in with his father-in-law, Preston Martin. They were always pulling jokes on Ben because he was a city boy. He came out of Fort Worth.

I never will forget Lester Stewart was quite a prankster. They were talking to Ben and somebody said, "I need a feather out of a buzzard wing sweep." They said, "Ben, have you got anything to do? No he did not have anything to do. Well, go over to Victor Scherer's Hardware and tell them that I need a feather out of a buzzard wing sweep. So Ben took off over to Victor Scherer's Hardware and Lester called ahead and told them, and he said, "Send him on to some other place." So he goes to Victor Scherer's Hardware and Victor said, "I don't have a feather anywhere in here from a buzzard swing sweep, but why don't you go over to Carter-Ivy Hardware and see if they have one."

Well, they called in advance, and there was three of four hardware stores in town. And they sent Ben to all of those stores. He came back and said,"I've been to every hardware store and I have not found a feather out of a buzzard wing sweep yet." I don't know if you know what a buzzard wing sweep was, but it was a sweep that you use in plowing and it's made out of metal. That's what a buzzard wing sweep was. BIG JOKE.

HARRY HAMER

I knew Harry quite well. You know, he had a little shop on York Avenue. I'd go by his place as I used to park over there at Milmo Lumber Co. after they closed down. Well, I started out one day, and old Harry had him a riding lawn mover, and there was a little box on the back of it. It looked like it was about 12-by-12 and about six inches deep. I asked Harry, "What's that box for? He said, "You know, I've got a lot of mowing to do out here Jack. I put me six cans of beer back there and a bunch of ice and I don't have to stop mowing to get me a can of beer. He was a character, Harry was.

CLINT HARDIN

As you know, Lester Stewart was our sheriff back in those days. Clint had lost a heel feeding a hay baler. He just barely got his foot out in time, and the plunger came along and cut his heel off. He walked on this toe on one foot. I believe it was his right foot.

Now Clint had done something here, and somebody filed some little charge, some misdemeanor of some sort, against Clint. And Clint found out about it, and he just sort of moved over to Fort Worth Well, one Sunday morning, early, Lester Stewart had gone to Fort Worth for something, and he was on his way back to Weatherford, and Clint was out there thumbing a ride. He was going to come over to Weatherford and spend the day. Lester recognized him, and he pulled up and opened – just reached over and opened the door and sort of turned around so Clint couldn't see who it was until Clint got in.Clint said, "Oh, my Lord, Lester, I wasn't looking for you." Well, the next day, Monday, they brought him down to my office, and – for whatever little thing it was – It wasn't anything serious. And I said,"Clint what in the world are you doing here?"

"Well," he said, "Jack, I've done a lot of hitchiking, but this is the first time I ever hitchhiked myself into jail." A lot of people were in jail for little old misdemeanors in those days.

JERRY LEE

And talking about old man Jerry Lee, you know he hauled milk in those days. I'm told they never stopped Jerry Lee during the milk strike. I think everyone thought he might have a shotgun with him. They said he was the only one who could get milk through. Jerry used to tell my dad, Sam Borden, about his son. Now his son was named Lecil but later on people called him Jerry. When the son, Lecil, was at Randolph Field in San Antonio, he would fly his plane up here and it had two seats in it. Lecil talked his dad, Jerry, into going up in the plane with him. Mr. Lee said "He rolled that plane, and I was flying upside down. I had a chew of tobacco in my mouth, and it hit me in the face three times before we got to the ground."

R. B. HOOD

I knew R. B. Hood, the Attorney, quite well. He was quite a criminal attorney. He would make the best speech of any man I think I've ever listened to. I used to listen to him argue, and I'd crawl out on the edge of my seat just listening to him.

I was just out of law school, and terms of court in those days were fall and spring terms. I got out in the spring, but didn't participate in any trials until the fall term. That would have been the fall term of 1936.

Well, the procedure in criminal cases is that the district attorney gets up and makes the first argument to the jury. Then the defense attorney gets up and makes his argument. And then the district attorney closes the argument. In other words the district attorney gets to open and close.

Well, I was Frank Fulgham's assistant when Frank was district attorney and it always evolved upon the assistant to make the opening argument. All you were supposed to do was go over the facts and let the jury know here are the facts and this and that. So I got up and made my argument and I told the jury that this is my first experience in the courthouse, the first trial I've ever participated in, had never made an argument before any jury, and if I don't do a very good job, why, just bear with me, I hope that I'll improve with time. And I thought I made a pretty good argument.

Well, Mr. Hood got up and he said, "Gentlemen of the jury…" That's before women were on the jury. "Gentlemen of the jury, I have told you, all along, that my client was not guilty. Now, that speech that Jack Borden made ought to be proof to you that he doesn't think the man is guilty."

He said, "Now, he tells you he's new at this business." But said, "I know that old country boy, and I've known him all his life. And if he'd believed this man was guilty, he wouldn't have been up here five minutes until he had that tie loosened. In ten minutes, he'd have had his coat off. In 15 minutes, he'd have been beating on this table and shouting at you." He said, "No, he was just calm and collected and didn't say anything. Now, that gentlemen, is an indication to me that Jack doesn't believe he's guilty either."

Well, I want to tell you, after that I talked loud and vociferously. They could hear me all the way to the railroad station down there. The windows were all up then. But that was my first experience with Mr. Hood. He had a keen mind.

In fact, someone had sold some mortgaged cattle, and we prosecuted him, and they got Mr. Hood to assist me in the prosecution. And we were talking to witnesses, and told them to tell us what they could testify to. So, we'd finally got them in and he said to the witnesses, "Now, I know I don't want to change your story, but if you'd speak in this manner, it gets over to the jury better." He knew what was going to get into the minds of the jurors.

But the best one that I know about him, Dick Belcher was a prosecutor over in the district next to us, and a nice, not overly-big fellow, and he wore a hat all the time. Now, Mr. Hood wore a size 8 hat, if you can imagine that. Well, Dick wore an ordinary sized hat, probably 7 1/8. And they were over there trying a lawsuit in Palo Pinto County, a criminal case. Now Dick got up and made his argument. Then Mr. Hood got up and started on his argument. Mr. Hood reached over to the hat rack and got Dick's hat and it just fit on the top of Mr. Hood's head, you know, that big old head of his. Now he says, "my young friend Dandy Dick." And he just went up one side and down the other on Dandy Dick.

Well, Dick Belcher was pretty sharp himself. He ended up on the Court of Criminal Appeals. So when he got back up, he said, "Well, you know, my friend, Mr. Hood, he reminds me of a story that I heard about these three brothers. They liked to hunt frogs, and one night one of the boys said to the other two, "Let's go frog hunting." No, we're to tired. He kept on. They said, "We're not going." He said, "Well, I'm just going by myself."

So he was gone a while and he came in about midnight and woke his brothers up and said. "Come out here in the yard – I want to show you the biggest bullfrog that you have ever seen." They said, "Hey, we've seen bullfrogs. We don't want to." He said, "Get up and come out here. This is a 42 pound bull frog." They said, "Forty-two pounds? There never was a bull frog that big." He said "You come on out here and see."

So the brothers got up and they went out in the yard and there was that big old bullfrog. And one of them said, "Well, that's the biggest frog I've ever seen, but he doesn't weigh any 42 pounds. He won't weigh over two pounds." And the brother told them, said, "Well it is two pounds of frog and 40 pounds of bull."

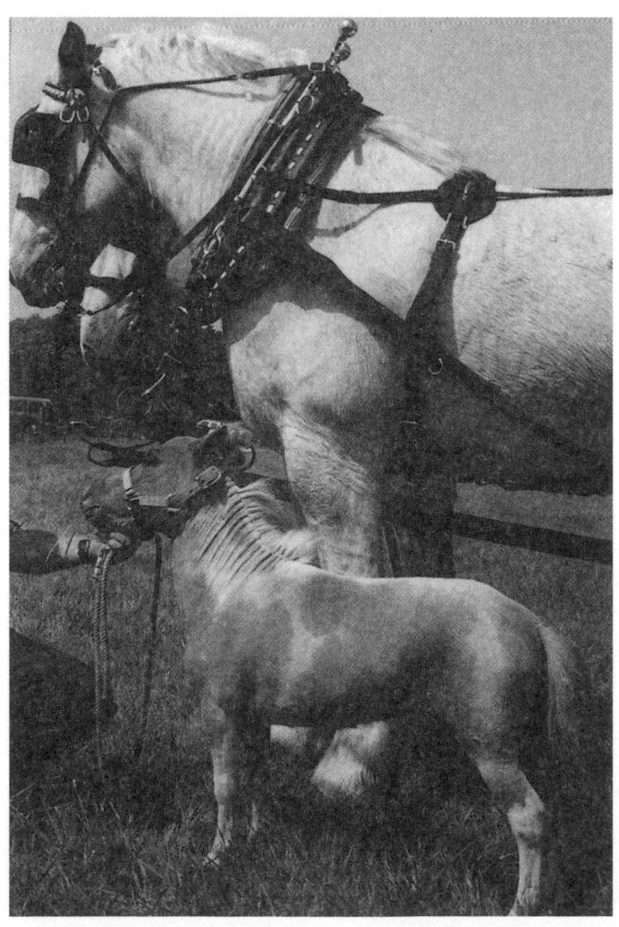

YOU JUST SUE AND BE DAMNED

R. B. Hood was one of the finest criminal lawyers, I guess, that there has been in Parker County, a tremendous speaker. When he was arguing on some civil case and I was local, I'd sit down there in the courtroom just to hear him talk. He was wonderful. He was a master of the English language.

One time there was a little ice condition in the county and he was on his way to Fort Worth. It was before the interstate and on U.S. 80 out there where it crossed Clear Fork, there was ice on the bridge. He met a man coming from the opposite direction on this bridge and they slowed down, and when they hit the brakes, why they started sliding and as a result, they ran into each other. They got out and they agreed that both of them were durn fools to be out on a day like that, and that each was equally liable and responsible, so they'd just pay for their own damage.

A few days later, this man appeared in Mr. Hood's office and said, "Well, I've been thinking about it and it was more your fault than it was mine, and I think you ought to pay for the damage to my car." Mr. Hood told him, he said, "You know, we agreed that both of us were foolish to be out on a day like that and I don't feel like I owe you anything and we agreed that we'd pay our own damages."The man said, "Well, if you don't pay me, I'm just going to sue you over in the courthouse." And Mr. Hood said, "My friend, I make my living in that courthouse and it holds no fear for me so you just sue and be damned. As far as I'm concerned, I'll be there." So the man didn't file a lawsuit.

COURT REPORTER SAM LITTLE

In the early days the court reporter didn't have a recording machine. I guess we didn't have them at that time. He took the testimony in shorthand and he'd sit there at that table and he'd have four or five tablets and a whole cup full of pens, because he'd run out of ink in one and he'd pick up another. Some of them had an ink stand up on the desk and they'd keep dipping in it. It was really a hard job because he sat there hour after hour and maybe a week or ten days, taking all this testimony.

Sam was a court reporter, and a good one. As I told a friend of mine later, I had three or four court reporter and I thought they were all just a little bit crazy to be doing something like that. But Sam put it down just like it was said.

We were trying a case up there, a criminal case, one time and we had some witnesses and they were talking about some Mexicans who were involved. One of these witnesses got up there and said, "now, them Mescans." And that's the way Sam put id down, and that's the way it came out in the transcripts, "them Mescans." That's the way it was in the old times. They didn't try to dress it down in any way. He was good. Sam died in 1955.

THE MCFARLANDS

The McFarlands had that big house out there on the hill where Kroger's is now. And we went out there frequently for dances. I never will forget, if my recollection is correct, the hard-wood floor was not your regular planks that you would ordinarily use, but they were squares. We used to go out there and have dances fairly frequently. We had a little old band here at the college that played some. I think that was the band that we had out there. Now, I could be mistaken. But we had some sort of music. I know that Louise and James Porter were just kids and we just had big times out there dancing. I danced with Louise, and I never could understand, as pretty a girl as she was, why she never got married. She is a great lady.

FRANK McENTIRE

My friend, Frank McEntire, owned a couple hundred acres out there just north of where Jerry's Chevrolet is now. And he had three or four old ponies out there. He and one of his friends were going to ride in the posse parade. Both of them were charter members. So they go out there to get the horses.

Frank said, "Hey, don't you think we ought to go on over to the line and get us a pint so that we'll have something to sort of fortify us in this ride?"

The friend said, "Yeah, that sounds like a good idea." So they went on over and got the pint of liquor. They were just getting ready to pull in the gate and Peck Nichols, who was commissioner in that precinct, came driving along. It was on old 80 before the interstate was built.

So Frank said, "Do you suppose old Peck would like to have a little drink?" And the friend said, "Well, I'll bet he would."

Of course, they both knew that Peck did drink a little. So the two went over there and Frank says, "Peck, we just wondered if you'd like to have a little drink?" And Peck says, "Well, yeah," So Frank pulled out the pint bottle that never had been opened, and handed it to Peck. Peck sets it over on the seat and says. "Thanks boys, I'd better wait until I get home to drink it." And he drove off. That trip to the line was wasted.

EDDLEMAN PICKARD

Eddleman Pickard was J. P. for sixteen years in Parker County. When he ran for J. P. the first time he really made a speech. He would say, "Now I am the only man in the race that can prove he's of sound mind." He would further state" that I have proof in my pocket from a hospital that I am of sound mind." He was a great person, a character, and made a great J. P.

After Eddleman got out, Homer Cantrell, I believe was the J.P. and then Sam Borden, my dad, ran against Homer and beat him, and Dad was J. P. for four years.

JOE QUANTE

Joe and his wife were traveling into Canada, and as they went through the customs there, the man said. "Mr. Quante, do you have any alcohol with you?" And Joe said "Yes I do."

Well, he said, "It's – you can buy it up here, but it's a violation of the law to carry it into Canada from the States." He said "You'll not be able to carry it with you."

Joe told me he had about half a pint. Joe said, "I asked him, Well, is there anything – is there any violation for me to take it in in my stomach?" The man said, "No sir."

Joe said, "I just uncorked the bottle and drank the whole thing." He was a great guy. Joe had a son Glenn, one of the nicest boys ever. Glenn was killed in WWII and Joe didn't ever get over Glenn's death. Joe's daughter, Juanita Wood, still lives in Weatherford.

W. D. NEWBERRY, Sr.

W. D. Newberry, Sr., father of Bill Newberry, started that insurance business from his home. He'd leave home at 5 o'clock in the morning. In those days, the farmers were up before daylight. They were ready to go to the fields at daylight. He'd drive, say to Peaster and Poolville, and he'd try to sell insurance and he built his business. He was a character.

His office was right down the stairs from us- when we were up over the M & F. Bank. And we all worked Saturdays in those days.

One Saturday afternoon about 3 or 4 o'clock in the afternoon, hot it was in the summertime, and I walked down to the foot of the stairs, and turned, and old Bill was sitting in there. The doors were open – you know, no air conditioning in those days – and he had his shoes off and his feet up on the desk. So I walked in the door and said in a pretty loud voice, "Bill Newberry, you ought to be ashamed of yourself. You're running a regular sweatshop here. You have these poor women, it's the middle of the afternoon, and you still got them in." He got his feet off that table and grabbed me by the arm and said, "Shut up, you durn fool. I have enough trouble with them as it is." He was my good friend.

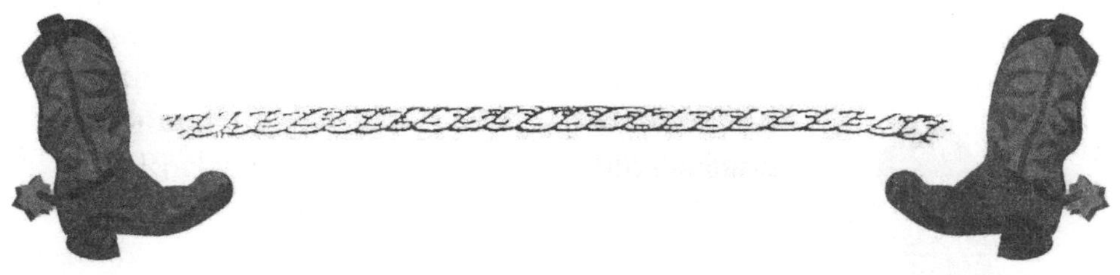

ANONYMOUS TALES OF THE PAST WITH JACK

BAD BREATH

Several years ago, I had a friend, well-known in Parker County, out on the east side of the county. He lived out close to Lake Weatherford, and I'd known him since I was a kid. They lived right down the creek from us.

He was prone to drink, sometimes more than he should. And he drove a truck, and one day, he was going home in his truck and a highway patrolman stopped him and pulled him over. The man says, "What are you stopping me for?" "Well, you were sort of weaving on the road. Have you been drinking?" And my friend said, "No, I haven't been drinking." And the highway patrolman said, "Well, what is that I smell on your breath?" "You know, I don't know. My wife's been complaining recently about how my breath smells bad." And so the patrolman let him go.

HOME-COURT ADVANTAGE

I was trying a case in the district court one time for a doctor, and I filed suit for him against some people. They employed a Fort Worth lawyer.

After we got the jury, the lawyer asked me, "Well, how many men of those jurors are the doctor's patients?" I said, "Well, there are six of them." He said, "How many are your clients?" I said, "Well, five of the other six are my clients." And he said, "Well, I guess I've got one that I can depend upon." And I said, "No, that young man is in Weatherford College and my wife is one of his instructors, and she's already told him that if I don't win, he doesn't pass." So we won the case. And this, of course, was appealed, and we got over there and the lawyer was up addressing the three justices on the court of appeals.

He told them that it was pretty hard for him to do anything in Parker County because six of those people on the jury were the doctor's patients, five of the other six were my clients, and that other boy went to school to my wife at Weatherford College, so he didn't have a whole lot of chance.

Well, one of the justicies – and this really happened – he broke up and said, "Well, that's a pretty envious position to be in, isn't it?" Evidently the three judges on the court of appeals were the doctor's patients, because we also won the court of appeal.

A BAD WAY TO SHOW UP FOR A TRIAL

When I was prosecuting attorney, I had a friend who was more or less retired; he was kind of a big rancher. He stayed around the courthouse a lot.

One of his neighbors was charged with DWI. My friend was in my office a day or two before the trial that came up on Monday. I said something about, well, the man was pretty well known to imbibe pretty freely and that if he got a bottle, why, he might be drunk when he came to his trial.

Apparently, my friend saw to it that his neighbor got a bottle early in the morning before he was supposed to appear. Ben Hagman was the defense attorney.

They called the case, and Ben said, "Judge, I don't know. My client's supposed to meet me here. I told him to be here before 9 a.m., but he hasn't shown up."

They went ahead with some other matters, and finally they called the case again. And Ben said, "Judge, I just don't know what happened to my client." The bench was on the east side of the courthouse, and the double doors were on the west part of the courtroom. And the hallway down from that went right straight into the judge's bench. The aisle must have been, oh, eight feet wide. And the judge said, "Now, Mr. Hagman, is that your client coming in?"

Here came the man, and he was just holding the bench on one side, and then on the other side. Ben got up and hauled him out of the courtroom. Ben came back in a little while and said, "Judge, we'll enter a plea of guilty a little later."

A FRIEND WORTH DRINKING FOR

Back in the days when I was prosecuting attorney, drunken driving – DWI – was a felony. The least sentence you could get would be a two-year sentence suspended, and it went from there up. Well, a good friend of mind was arrested on a DWI charge by a good friend of his. My friend was a truck driver, and the deputy sheriff or policeman, whichever he was, had been a driver for him. We had to try him, and the jury found him guilty and gave him a suspended sentence. Well, my friend – I lost his friendship over this, and he blamed me for it. This was back in the day, oh, say, 1939 or '40.

After the Sheriff's Posse was organized – it was organized in '47. Well, along came '48, '49, '50, or something like that, and the Sheriff's Posse was riding in the Mineral Wells parade for their show they were going to put on. And this friend of mine hauled the horses over there for those who didn't have trailers or something. And they parked the truck up there beyond the Crazy Hotel, on that street right across from the Crazy Hotel. And there was a beer joint there.

Well, we got on our horses and we all rode down to the parade grounds where it was going to start. So, this truck owner said, "I need to go back and get my truck, because here's where I'm going to load them when we get through with this parade. Somebody needs to take me."

Now my car was there and my wife was over there, so I said, "I'll take you up there." And he hesitated and hesitated. And I said, "Come on, I'll take you up there." We got back there where that truck was, and there was a beer joint right across the street. And I said, "Bud, let's go over here and get us a bottle of beer." So we went over there and we sat down. And I told him, "Now, you've been unhappy with me ever since your DWI. And I want to tell you that I, and your friend the deputy sheriff, we didn't have anything we could do besides enforce the law, and there's nothing personal about it. I just wanted to let you know, and I wanted to tell you now that there's not anything that we did that we didn't have to do." I said, "Did you ever get that dismissed? Then you got a suspended sentence and after the two years is up, or whatever it was, you could go back in and tell the court, 'Hey, I've been clean.' "And the court would dismiss it and it could never be brought against you at any other time." I said, "Have you ever had that done?" He said no. And I said, "I'll tell you what: Monday morning, you come to my office and you and I will go up before Judge Carter and we'll get that removed." And I never had a better friend after that.

I told my Sunday School Class this when I was the teacher, and some of them said, "You mean you sat down and had a can of beer with him?" I said, "I'd drink anything with him to get his friendship back. That beer didn't hurt me, but it hurt me to lose a friend." This actually happened. After that, until he died, I never had a better friend.

A BOOTLEGGER'S LOVE OF PARKER COUNTY

A man moved because I was going to prosecute him for bootlegging. I had told him, "Now, you're going to jail for 100 days or else you're going to move out of Parker County, whichever you want to do." And he said, "OK." That was not long before I went into the FBI. Well, I didn't come back home for, oh, almost two years after I went into the FBI. When I did, I walked down to the Texas Café, and one of the first persons I saw was my friend. And I said, "Friend, what are you doing here?" He said, "Well, I live here now." I said, "I thought that you and I had an agreement you were going to move out of town and you weren't going to come back."

"Well, he said, "when Mr. Queen was appointed county attorney, I figured y'all would let me come back, so I've been back ever since."

SEEKING SAFE SHELTER

I had a custody case about a child, a little boy, about three years old. A fine-looking little boy. Well, not long after the case was over, I started home one day, and I met the father on a motorcycle, and he had that little boy on there with him.

I called him up Monday morning, and I said, "Son, if I ever see you with that boy on that motorcycle again, I'm going to go to court on my own and tell them that you're not a fit father, to take the child away from you and give him to somebody that will take care of him."

THE DANGERS OF PLEASING EVERYONE

I've always tried to please everybody if I could. I'm sort of like a story I heard not long ago.

An old man and a little boy were going to town. They had a donkey and the little boy was riding it. They met some people on the road, and one of them said, "Well, it's a shame for that old man to have to walk while that little boy is sitting on the donkey." The man and boy thought about it and said, "Maybe you're right." So the old man got on the donkey and the little boy walked. People said, "Well, what a shame for that old man to ride that donkey and have the little boy walk."

The child and old man discussed it and decided they'd both walk. Then they turned and met some other people who said, "Well, look at that, isn't that a shame. There's a good, strong-looking donkey and that man and boy are both walking. Why don't they both ride the donkey?" So they both rode the donkey.

Well, in a little while they met some other people, and they said, "My goodness gracious. What a shame – that old man and that little boy riding that poor little old donkey. That is absolutely a shame." So the two got off. They decided, "Well, OK. We'll do it better." So they got to carrying the donkey. Well, they got to the river bridge and they started across it and lost control of the donkey. It fell into the river and drowned. The moral of the story is, if you try to please everybody, you'll end up losing your … donkey.

QUOTES FROM FAMILY AND FRIENDS OF JACK BORDEN

Bailey and Hannah Kathryn Burks:

It seems Jack Borden has two little neighbors that love him very much. And of course there is a reason. It seem that practically since the children were born, Jack has brought them lots of popcorn. So – the name they call him is: POPCORN JACK.

Sherry Jackson:

Just a note – I admire Mr. Jordan tremendously

Dorothy Thomas Pearce:

I have known Mr. Borden since I was a teenager as he took care of my dad's business (Angie Thomas) and he has been our lawyer since 1961 and he is now our daughter's lawyer. He has always given sound advice in all matters. Early to the office for time and prayer and the Bible – He took time to select the right path and then proceeded to make a way.

Jenny Barnwell:

I have so many fond memories of Jack. When I was the probate auditor for Parker County, my favorite times in court were the days that Jack was representing someone. He always had a story to tell about some elected official or another attorney he had worked with in the past. We would all be in stitches before he left the courtroom. He is one of the best.

Bud and Betsy Dearing:

We have known Mr. Borden for many years and have found him to be a most generous person. We have not read the book, but in our dealings with him, have found him to represent all the things we have submitted in the title contest.

Jerry Newberry:

Jack Borden is truly a remarkable person and unforgettable character!

Morris White:

When Morris White was a young boy his father and mother, Charlie and Evelyn White, owned and operated an auto repair shop on the corner of York Ave. and Spring St. It was called C. A. White & Sons. On the south side of the shop there was a side door that opened on to Spring St. Right across Spring St. was where Jack Borden entered his law office. Now Morris and his brother, Larry, really liked Jack Borden and he was the family lawyer. Sometimes Morris would take a high-pressure water hose and spray just behind Jack as he walked up the street to enter his office thru a side door. He did not really get Jack wet but he did make him rush a little to get out of the way and sometimes a little water might have reached him. Now Jack was good to Morris and did not tell on him " every time." However, after reporting him a time or two he would threaten to tell on him again. Anyway the White family, including Morris, has always appreciated Jack very much. Morris also reports that his little "water joke" did not go over to well with some other lawyers who walked the same path to work.

Coy Carter:

Jack Borden, in my opinion, is one of the finest lawyers in Parker County or anywhere else. And I should know. He was my advisor the many years I was Sheriff. He probably kept me out of jail. I have watched his action in the courtroom. He was shrewd but kindhearted. He always found the time to talk with anyonc at any time. I have always considered him my friend. I was talking with him at his home one day in the yard and he mentioned he needed a certain kind of glove to work in the yard with and he just could not find them. I told him I would get him some and I did. When I gave them to him I told him I really felt sorry for his wife as I knew she would be the one using them – not him.

C. B. Borden:

Jack was 17 and never worked anywhere but the family farm. Farming went by the wayside and our father, Sam, took his two boys, Jack and C. B., to Yuma Arizona to seek work. They stayed out there four years before returning to Weatherford. Jack decided he wanted to pursue college and everyone said he wouldn't stay, as he was after all just a farm boy. He got a job selling and delivering ice and in a couple of years he had worked his way through the junior college. He then decided he wanted to go to Austin and get a law degree at the University of Texas. Once again everyone told him he would never last and should just go on back to the farm because that's all he really knew. The only people who knew his determination, was his family. Anyone who knows Jack knows that he is a little stubborn and he went anyway. Three years later he had his degree and was ready to practice law. Weatherford is an old town with a lot of old lawyers and everyone told him he was wasting his time trying to settle in this town. With that said he ran for the county attorney and won. He held this position for two and a half years and then went to work for the FBI for four years. When he returned home he opened his own law firm and Jack was able to succeed as a prosperous attorney. You can always tell a good hunter by the number of pelts he carries and Jack has a lot of pelts. All of this is true and I could tell you lots more because he has been my brother for ninety -one years.

Barbara A. Edwards

I moved from California to Weatherford in 1975, and in, March, 1983, started work at Borden and Westoff. I soon discovered Mr. Borden knew well my Weatherford relatives, as well as my mother in California. One early morning he called me in his office to introduce me to his brother, C. B., who also knew the family, but at the end of the conversation, Mr. Borden told C. B., "Now, C. B., she's not like the rest of the Coopers – they were quiet people!" It seems he had come to know me well! Mr. Borden has an amazing memory, and always a story or anecdote to bring your spirits up. He is a wonderful boss, as well as friend. To him I am grateful, and for him I have much admiration and respect.

Leon Tanner:

Back in the 30's or 40's Leon Tanner and a bunch of his friends were sort of (maybe a whole lot of) mischievous. Leon remembers one time he was pushing the friends to do something a little worse than usual. His friends told him he was trying to get them all thrown in jail. Now threat of jail did not scare him, as Jack Borden was a family friend. He advised the others that if they get in jail, just call Jack and he will get them out or get in with them. He still tells people everywhere he goes that his "No fear of Jail" is still with him as he knows Jack Borden can fix anything.

Dr. Noel Bryan:

Noel Bryan remembers when he was captain of the "Posse" in 1988. Now he and the entire posse wanted to honor their charter members. Noel cannot remember who all the charter members were but he does remember that Jack Borden was one of them and what was to be a great event in front of the usual great rodeo crowd was a near catastrophe. A horse drawn stagecoach of some sort was brought in and all the Charter Members were to be loaded in and driven around the arena with much fan fare. Everything was going well until for some unknown reason, as the gentlemen were ready to enter the stagecoach, the horses decided to run away – around and around the arena they went. No one was hurt, but one cowboy inside the arena was nearly injured as the horses nearly pinned him against the fence. Noel does not remember all the details, but he does remember how thankful he was that none of the Charter Members, or anyone else, was injured. Jack will probably remember the details and come up with a funny story.

Stacy Baker:

I have worked for Mr. Borden for 3 ½ years and can say that he is the most caring person that I have ever met. He is a very special man and means the world to me. He truly cares about and does what he can to help people. I am honored and blessed to say that I have worked for and know such a wonderful man.

Walter F. Worthington:

When I worked at First National Bank of Weatherford in the late 1960's, Bank Director Jack Borden was on the Loan & Discount Committee and we met every ten days to review the loans that had been granted during that period of time. We met at 7:00 A. M. at Jack's insistence. The meetings were supposed to last one hour but Bank President W. Felix Jones, who was quite a story teller, would usually have a story about several of the loans and maybe even a story or two that did not pertain to any loans. Therefore, the meetings would many times be on the verge of running overtime. Jack would begin to get fidgety after about forty-five minutes and would say, "Felix, let's get this meeting over, I have to go to work" and when Jack said this, he was downright adamant about it. Felix would then try to accommodate him and finish the meeting on time, but at 8:00 A. M., Jack left whether the meeting was over or not. After all, he had plenty of clients and plenty of work and he wanted to get at it.

Charles C. Brinkley:

I have known Jack Borden for all my life. I knew him when growing up on the East Side of town and got to know him better after going to work in the Merchants & Farmers State Bank in Weatherford, February 1, 1945. Jack was always jolly when he came into the bank and seemed to always have time to chat no matter how busy he might have been. I had him do legal work for us during the 10 years I was Vice President at the First National Bank in Weatherford. It was also a pleasure to work with Jack as a bank director. His counsel and input was always done in good taste and was extremely helpful.

Jack and his lovely wife are members of the First Baptist Church in Weatherford. The last time I was asked to sing for a Sunday School Department at that church about five years ago, Jack Borden was there. He is still practicing law and is still very good at what he does. It was my pleasure to also know his father, Sam Borden. Sam was also a colorful character in his own way. Jack is one of the most unforgettable people it has been my pleasure to know.

Jessie McMeekin:

I have been with Jack Borden's law firm for 30 years. The last 15 years of that time as his secretary. He is a Christian and a Good Samaritan and believes in helping churches as well as individuals. As we all know, he is full of funny stories and loves to visit with his clients. He is good at solving problems and encourages us to do what is right. We just thank the Good Lord we have been privileged to know and work with him.

Lori Tollett:

I have had the great pleasure of working for Jack Borden for the past fifteen years. He is a remarkable man, with countless stories to tell about his life and history growing up in Parker County. He is so very dedicated and loyal to his many clients and friends, making him such an asset to his profession and this community.

Billy R. Cain:

When I first ran for Sheriff in 1976, Mr. Borden gave me some good advise that was: Never promise more than you can deliver. I am retired sheriff of Parker Co.

Shawna Gentry:

In the few years I have known Mr. Borden, he has greatly influenced my life. Passion for his profession. Loyalty and love for his wife. Dedication and respect for his friends and staff. This is what makes knowing and working for Mr. Borden such an honor. To the man who taught me the meaning of "Yellow Dog Democrat."

Herb Fowler:

When I was young my relatives told me we were ken to Jack Borden who was an established lawyer already. I'm not sure if it is true on how we are related on my mother's side (Wallis). My wife's family (Joann Harrell) grew up with the Sam Borden family and told how they swam with them in the Brazos River. She told me of good things they did for her family and others. I know even today whether in his office or at church, it is always interesting and entertaining to talk to Jack.

Don Huff:

When I think of Jack Borden, words such as honor, dignity, wisdom, selflessness and modesty all come to mind. Jack has provided tireless dedication, unending commitment and service to Weatherford College and to this community. His law firm is responsible for securing the largest gift to Weatherford College in the history of the institution. He is a graduate of Weatherford College and is the type of supporter that any college would want for an alumnus. He gives of himself far above and beyond any expectations. On a personal note, I admire his wit and humor and appreciate his down-to-earth approach to life. He is an inspiration to me, and a real pleasure to know.

Ben Whiteman, Jr.

When I became Sheriff in 1989, Mr. Borden was one of the first Sheriff's Posse members to call and welcome me to the organization. He has always been a friend of law enforcement and ready to assist us when we needed a helping hand. Congratulations on your book.

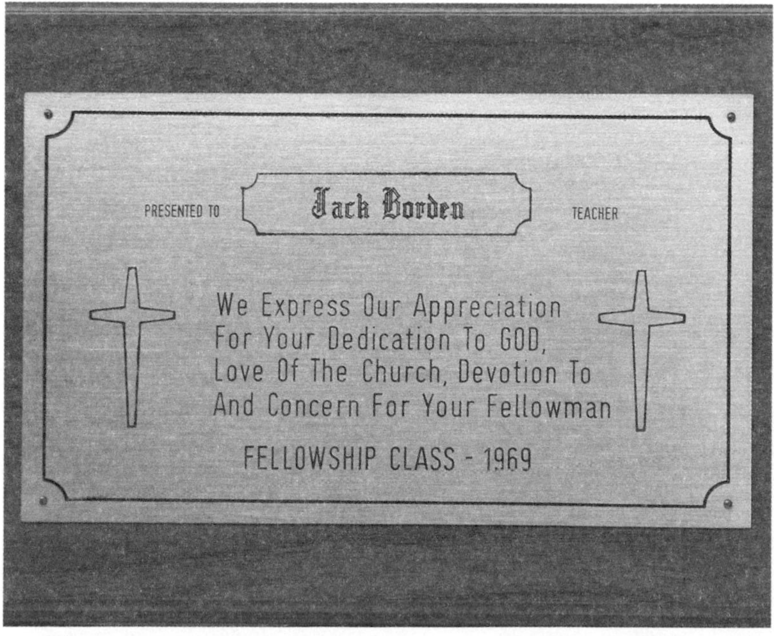

Boley and Evelyn Pearson:

Many years ago we'd meet in Red River. The Borden's would always stay two weeks and we stayed one week, at Hickman's up Bitter Creek Canyon. We always did a lot of fishing and were lucky catching fish. Many times in the evening we would cook our fish. Jack would cook potatoes and onions and we'd fry the fish. Everyone in the Lodge was jealous because they could smell the fish cooking. Some mornings Jack and Boley would get up at daylight and catch their limit, go back to the cabin, wake the girls up and have breakfast. Then about mid morning we would go out and visit with our neighbors, who were fishing, and many questions and fish stories took place.

While cooking bacon one morning, Jack asked Evelyn if she thought the sty-ro-foam cup would hold the bacon drippings and she said probably since it holds hot coffee. Jack poured the drippings and the cup disintegrated – The mess that made - made an unhappy Jack.

We started taking our five grandsons, Stan, Brian, John, Cris and Paul on our trips to Red River. One night, Stan, suggested we have a picnic. Jack and Edith were pleased to roast hotdogs and Stan made s'mores consisting of graham cracker, chocolate and marshmallows. Jack loved to tease Brian. Sometimes Jack would call him "Sorry Dang Boy", so Brian would say, "Sorry Dang Jack." Boley would correct Brian, but it was too funny to stop. John liked to visit Jack and Edith and would go knocking on their door at all hours. We told them to just send him away but they would invite him in for breakfast. The boys learned a lot from Edith and Jack.

One time Edith, Linda, Pam and Evelyn went to Greeley, Colorado to visit her brother and family. Jack and Boley stayed in Red River to fish. We went through Leadville and Central City on the way. We were late returning from our trip and Jack was worried if anything happened, all of our identification would be in Weatherford and they'd be in Colorado. Great Times.

Wendolyn Stroud:

Mr. Borden and I are life long Parker County residents and our families were friends. We also attend the same Church, therefore we have a conversation most every day about someone we both know. My life has been enriched by working with Mr. Borden the past 11 years. He is a very popular attorney who has many clients and friends. Some drive miles to use his services or just to visit with him. He is a "One of A Kind" and has "Certainly made a difference in this World."

Phil Livingston:

Jack Borden is an old-time Texas lawyer, a man who has always been a credit to his profession and a person to "ride the river with." A Weatherford native, Borden has lived in the town his entire life, commenting once that "my family came to town back when it was a wide spot in the road serving as a supply center for trail herds heading north to Kansas.' The man has been a strong supporter of his community during his long career, a former Mayor, and early member of the Parker County Sheriff's Posse, a participant in civic growth and has always been ready to 'give back' to the town which has nurtured him. He is always good company to be around and has a wry sense of humor, which includes his tales about the size of the fish he's caught on one of his vacation jaunts. It has been a privilege knowing him.

Richard Sharpe"

Jack Borden was a long time director of the First National Bank of Weatherford. About 1975, the local owners of First National sold the bank to a group of investors from Ft. Worth headed by a prominent Ft. Worth banker. The new group announced that all directors over the age of 65 would have to retire from the board. Now a majority of the board fell in the "over 65" category. None took it well but all complied. A while after the "old timers" left the board, Edith Borden went into the bank and asked someone at the customer service counter for a small favor which in the past had been gladly provided. The customer service officer did not know Mrs. Borden and told her that the bank could not accommodate the request. Mrs. Borden explained that she was Mrs. Jack Borden and that her husband had been a long-time director. The bank employee still refused the request. Mrs. Borden was upset and when Jack came home for lunch, she told Jack that she wanted him to call the bank president and tell him what had happened so it would not happen again. Jack's reply was "Now Edith, over in Exodus it says, "There arose a King in the land that knows not Joseph", and now it seems there has arisen a King in Parker County that knows not the Borden's.

Bill David who was a partner in the Ft. Worth law firm of Cantey and Hanger told me that when he tried a case in Parker County, he always got Jack Borden to help him pick the jury. On one occasion, the trial was considered a "big one" and the district courtroom was full of prospective jurors. Bill David arose and asked the jury panel if there was anyone present who did not know Jack Borden. One lone hand was raised. Mr. David said he was shocked that there was even one and so he asked "You don't know Jack Borden?" No sir was the reply. Mr. David then asked "How long have you lived in Parker County?" Six months was the reply.

About 1998, Jack was helping me with a land transaction in Parker County and I was in his office. I said, "Jack, I see you are still chewing tobacco." He said, "Yeah, when Edith and I were going to get married, she made me promise that I would stop chewing tobacco, and I did for Six Months." Jack went on," You know Richard they have been telling me for years that chewing tobacco was going to kill me" and I finally found out what they meant. Dub Jordan and I and our wives had been out to New Mexico and we were coming back on I-10. My chaw was used up and it needed changing. I keep my tobacco in a plastic bag. I held it with one hand and reached for a chaw, and I realized I didn't have a hand on the steering wheel?

Jack served in the FBI during World War II. He delighted in getting in an elevator with a fellow FBI agent and saying in the crowded elevator, "You know that was the worst murder scene I can remember." He then added plenty of juicy details about the murder. By the time the elevator stopped everyone got off and followed Jack down the hall as he continued to give gory details in a loud voice. Of course there was no murder. He had probably been only doing dull "lawyer work" in the office.

Dick Layman:

Jack has always been a good friend and a fine brother-in-law. He is a good man.

Terri Short:

Uncle Jack was always the kind man with the booming voice. He always had a smile and I loved sitting on his lap. I can still remember his big hands reaching down to pick me up. I am in awe of all he has accomplished in his life and how full of energy he still remains, I hope I got those genes!!!

Sammye Borden Layman:

Jack really is a terrific brother. I guess I adored him from the time I was old enough to "see" him, since he was 16 years older than I was. When I was young, he could do no wrong. When I was about 5, I remember, I followed Jack everywhere I could and he took me lots of places with him – but he wouldn't ever let me go on a date with him !! (I couldn't understand that)

Jack went off to the University of Texas. When I was nine, I remember one weekend when he came home he brought his typewriter to do a paper. I was fascinated with his ability to type. I asked him how he did that and he told me he had eyes in his fingers and of course I believed him and for year's I tried to find them.

Do you know how hard it is to have two fathers? – Yes, Jack appointed himself my second one when I became a teen-ager. Jack was District Attorney when I was in high school and he would try to keep tabs on me. If I was going to town after school I always made sure my mother knew it and it was okay, because the minute I got to the square, somehow, Jack always saw me and would call Mother and "squeal" on me.

There are lots of wonderful memories of my brother, I am not able to share them all, but ask Jack about being arrested on his honeymoon!

Bill Jordan:

Man in the Hat- It is hard to decide which you notice first- The warm smile or the Trademark Fedora Hat. But one thing you know for certain is that both will be waiting to welcome and greet you, along with his friendly handshake. As you enter the First Baptist Church for Sunday morning Bible Study, Jack Borden has been greeting people, each by name, as they arrive for class for as long as I can remember. What a wonderful way to start your Sunday morning. Thank You, Jack.

CONTEST

To Name The Book

George Kinback:
"Tell Me A Law Story, Jack"

C. B. Borden:
"Beating the Odds, Life and Times of a Parker County Farm Boy"

Linda Hargrave:
"The Life of The Infamous Attorney"
"The "Crack of Dawn" Attorney"

Loree Ellis:
"The Life of a Parker County Lawyer"
"Jack Borden, Country Lawyer"
"Life Stories Of A Country Lawyer"

Scott BrumBach:
"Borden's Old School of Law"
"Borden's Law"
"Jack's Law"
"Jack's Verdict"
"The Trials of Jack Borden"
"Country Law by Jack Borden"
"Country Law – 1936"

Ruth F. Wiley:
"The Last Texas Lawman"

Carl Elder"
"Plow A Strait Furrow"
"The Life and Times of a Country Lawyer"

Bud and Betsy Dearing:

"Counsel With A Conscience"
"A Lawyer With A Heart"
"A Common Man's Friend"

Karen Steward:

"Parker County; We've Got Jack"
"Parker County Through The Eyes Of JackBorden"
"Parker County: Through The Eyes of Jack"
"Parker County And The Life Of Jack Borden"
"Parker County! The Life and Law of Jack Borden"
"Jack Borden, Life of a Lawyer in Parker County"
"Jack Borden, Longtime Lawyer of Parker County"
"Jack Borden, Parker County's Lawyer"
"Jack Borden: The Tales of Law in Parker County"
"Jack Borden, Biography of a Parker County Lawyer"
"Longevity, Law, and the Love for Parker County as told by Jack Borden"
"Memoirs of Jack Borden, Parker County Lawyer"
"Memoirs: Parker County and Jack Borden"
"Memoirs: The History of Law in Parker County"
"Reminiscing the Life of Jack Borden"
"Parker County Lawyer"
"REFLECTION: "A Look into the Life of a Parker County Lawyer"

Dorothy Reynolds:

"The Tales of Whispering Sam's Son"

Joel Causey:

"Living, Learning, Laughing with Jack Borden, Country Lawyer"

Jessie McMeekin:
"Jack Borden, Attorney, to Whom Service to Clients is More Important than Fee"

Wendolyn Stroud:
"Tales of a Texas Lawyer"

J. Causey:
"JACK, Reflections of a Country Lawyer"

Linda Heatly:
"Tales of a Dad-Burn Lawyer"

Louis Washburn:
"JACK BORDEN "A Chance to Look Back"

Jo Ann Causey:
"Life and Times of A Country Lawyer: The Jack Borden Story"

Carl Causey:
"A Lifetime to Remember: Perspective from a Country Lawyer"

Martha Lewis:
"The Life and Times of a Texas Lawyer"

J. K. and Wilma Jean Johnson:
"I've Seen It All"
"Wisdom by Jack"
"Life and Times of Jack Borden"
"Friend to All"
"Servant and Friend"

Charlene Fowler Moyer:
"Parker County From the Old Boar's Nest"

James W. Key:

"A Parker Patriot"

Jenny Barnwell:

"A Parker County Legend - The Story of Jack Borden"

"Ode to a Legend – The Jack Borden Story"

"Still Standing Tall – The Life of Jack Borden"
"Attorney at Law"

"The Legendary Jack Borden –
A Historical Review of his Life in Parker County"

"An Old West Adventure – The Life and Times of Jack Borden"

"Through The Eyes of Jack – The Life and History of Parker County"

"94 Years Later – A Historical Review of Parker County"

"So Many Stories To Tell"

"Parker County's Best – Attorney, Comedian and Historian"

"Reflections – The Stories of Jack Borden, Attorney @ Law"

Sharon K. Mims:

"We sure were Characters!"

"Jack Borden's Reminiscences of Parker County and its People'"

"From Clear Fork to Weatherford"
"Recollections of a Lifelong Parker County Lawyer"

"My Journey From Clear Fork to Weatherford"
"Recollections of a Lifelong Parker County Lawyer"

"I Had a Lot of Friends"
"Recollection of Longtime Parker County Lawyer and Public Servant Jack Borden"

"Jack Borden" "Parker County Attorney-at-law"

Doris Wright Kinback:

"Life stories of 94 years"

"Jack Borden Attorney at Law"

"The Man for All Times"

"The Extraordinary Life Of Jack Borden"

"Parker County Attorney-at-law"

"The Man for All Times"

"THE MAN"

"Times and Life of Jack Borden

"Parker County Attorney-at-law"

"VERDICT – JACK BORDEN

"Parker County Attorney-at-law

The "Man" for all times"

Wanda Lovelace:

"Jack Borden – Lawyer with a Heart"

"Jack Borden – A Good Man and a Lawyer"

Pam Lee:

"A Man of Many Hats"

"Parker County's Man of Many Hats"

Bob Glenn:

"The County Counselor"

"Reflections of a Country Lawyer"

Kathy Densmore:

"Got Milk! NO " - "Law! – YES"

MR. BORDEN

Freddy Detherage:

"Jack Borden, The Best Parker County Lawyer"

Pat Haddock:

"A Parker County Attorney Remembers WHEN—"

Verda Detherage:

"Need a Lawyer, Call Jack Borden"

James Haddock:

"Life and Trials of a Parker County Attorney"
"Memories of a Parker County Attorney"

Boley and Evelyn Pearson:

"Tales of an Old Country Lawyer"
"The Life and Times of an Old Country Lawyer"
"Jack Borden – A Country Lawyer's Story"
"Jack Borden – Lawyer, Extraordinaire"
"Jack Borden , A Country Lawyer on Jack Borden"
"Footprints of Jack Borden in the ages gone by"
"Tracing the Footprints of Jack Borden"
"Appointment with Jack Borden"
'Father Time and Jack Borden"
"Footprints of Time in the Life of Jack Borden"
"JACK BORDEN, A LEGEND IN HIS TIME"
"A Whole Body of Stories by Jack Borden"

James D. Lamb:

"A Longhorn at Work"

RANDI WHEELER; (A winner) **********

"BOOTS and BRIEFCASES "

Bob Glenn:

"Parker County President"
"Parker County Statesman"
"Parker County Legend"

Pat Haddock:
"Parker County's Ageless Attorney"

Oleane Parten:
"The 6 A.M. Workhorse"

J. B. Parten:
"Mirror of a Strong Man"

Rita Stinson:
"Reflections of Jack's Love"

Jerry Newberry:
"Jack Borden, A Country Lawyer Defined"

James D. Lamb:
"A Longhorn at Work"
"The Life and Times of a Longhorn"

Doris Dossey:
"A Texas Gentleman"

Wayne Thompson:
"Local Boy Makes Good for Everyone"
"A Great Man"

Donna Couch:
"Pass the Chaw"

Walter Couch:
"Sit a Spell with Jack"

Dr. Noel Bryan:
"A Country Barrister"

Dorothy Pearce:
"Country Lawyer-Pathfinder- Waymaker"

WANDA TODD – (A Winner) **************
"Toils, Trials and Tales of a Texas Attorney"

Billy Cain:
"Trials and Trails of a Texas Lawyer
By Jack Borden Attorney at Law"

Walkene Larkin:
"Memoirs of a Parker Co. Lawyer"
"Memorabilia of Jack Borden"
"Memoirs of a Small Town Lawyer"
"Parker Co. Legend: Jack Borden Attorney At Law"
"Life and Times of Jack Borden"

Evelyn Ellis:
"Happy Moments"

Sherry Jackson:
"The Gentleman from Parker County"

Gene Burks:
"POPCORN JACK'
"You Don't Know Jack"

Vickie Combs:
"The Journey of a County Attorney"

Ben Combs:
"A Journey Into The Past"

Tracy Mansell:
"All about The House That Jack Built"
"The House That Jack Built"
"What About Jack?"
"You Don't Know Jack-But Here's Your Chance"
"The House That Jack Built,
The Life of Jack Borden"

Colton Tollett:
"Looking out a Window through an old Buzzard's Eye"

Chelsea Tollett:
"The Life and Times of an old Parker County Buzzard"

Judy Kemp White:
"Lawyer Jack Borden"
"Parker County Famous Verdicts in
Weatherford Wins"
"Parker County Lawyer – Jack Borden"
"Watermelon to Peaches"
"Parker County Lawyer – Jack Borden"
"Watermelons to Peaches in 62 Years"
"Country Bumpkin Lawyer"
"Parker County Famous Jack Borden"

Mr. And Mrs. John Campbell:
"The Eyes of Texas Law"
"67 Years of a Country Lawyer"
"Texas Law On The Square"
"67 Years of a Country Lawyer"

Dick Layman:

"Jack Borden – The Best Friend Parker County Ever Had"
"Jack Borden – Parker County's Prize"

Terri Short:

"The Life of a Legend"
"The Life and Times of a Parker County Lawyer"
"A Look at a Great "Law" Man"
"The Life of a Great "Law" Man"

Sammye (Borden) Layman:

"Jack Borden – A Legend In His Own Time"
"Jack Borden – A Legend of Parker County"
"The Pride Of Parker County"

Trena Poe:

"Jack Borden The Man, The County, The Legand"

Margaret Todd:

"Parker County Lawyer"

In Conclusion

Jack states: One of my favorite stories is – and I think it will be a good conclusion to this book – one Sunday morning a Baptist preacher told his congregation that he wanted them to assist him in preaching the sermon. They wanted to know what in the world they could do to help.

He said, "Well, I'm going to say a word, and I want you all to sing a hymn that comes to mind. Now, do you get it?"

And they said, "Yes" He said, "Cross"
So they all started singing,
"The Old Rugged Cross."
He said, "That's good. Now, Grace."
They started singing, "Amazing Grace."
"Oh," he said. "You all are just doing wonderful.
Then he said, "Blood." And they all started singing, "Power in the Blood."
Then he said, "Sex".
There was a deathly silence.

In the back, there was an old couple, 87–year old man and his 86-year-old-wife. They got up and, at the top of their voices started singing the song, "Precious Memories."

2003
To be continued?

We continue in 2008 as we promised in 2003, when Jack Borden was 95 years old. The following pages detail his activities and honors from 2003 to 2008 when he turned 100 years old.

Nebo Valley Press
Leon Tanner & Mary Kemp

Local charities to benefit from this 2nd printing with additions.

Jack Borden
Activities and Honors
2003-2008

After the publication of this book, in 2003, Jack Borden received the Alumnus of the Year Award from Weatherford College. He had already received the Distinguished Alumnus Award and the Carlos Harnett Award. Jack was the first person to receive all of these major awards from Weatherford College.

Early in 2004, he became co-host of a radio program on KYQX Weatherford station. The program featured history from all the communities in Parker County, Texas. It was originated and hosted by Jamie Bodiford - Brinkly. The program is still on the air each Friday morning and Jack still makes appearances on the program.

In 2005 Jack received the Weatherford Chamber of Commerce, Outstanding Citizen Award, for loyalty, time and talent that he gave, to serve the community in Parker County, Texas. This award is a very coveted award in Parker County and Weatherford, TX. This was quite a surprise for Jack – We watched him almost become speechless. Ha! The Outstanding Citizen Award has been given for 55 years. Jack Borden joins the ranks of recipients including: Mary Martin, Jim Wright and Larry Hagman.

In 2007 at a Sheriff's Posse Clubhouse meeting, he received a plaque evidencing 60 years of service in the Parker County Sheriff's Posse. Jack was also recognized as the oldest living member of the Sheriff's Posse in Parker County.

Some of Jack's friends had a birthday party for him at the Parker County Sheriff's Posse Clubhouse on Mineral Wells Hwy on his 100th birthday on August 5, 2008. The crowd was estimated at 500 people and he received over 250 birthday cards. Among the speakers were Jim Wright, former speaker of the House of Representatives in Washington D.C. and Bob Glasgow, State Senator from Stephenville, Texas. Jack stated that after listening to part of the things they had to say about him he decided he must be at the wrong party, that maybe he was at someone else's birthday party.

On July 16th, 2008, Jack received an invitation, from the special agent in charge of the Dallas headquarters of the Federal Bureau of Investigation. He was invited to attend the July 21st celebration of the 100th birthday of the FBI. Unbeknown to Jack when he dictated a letter to Rose telling them that he would not be able to attend, that she would write, "this old man would dearly love to come but he is not physically able to drive over there. If, he had a way there he would be delighted to come." On Friday, 18th he received a phone call, Rose answered and replied, Jack the FBI is going to pick us up at 7:00p.m. on Monday, July 21st to take us to the FBI's 100th Anniversary Celebration. Jack and Rose attended the Celebration and went to all the meetings and heard Kay Bailey Hutcheson, gave a speech about the FBI. Jack was seated in the V.I.P. row. When she completed her speech, the agent in charge got up and said, "There is one other person I want to introduce to you. We have with us the oldest living, former FBI member, Jack Borden. Jack is 99 years old. Jack said, " I was not only astonished but was delighted at what had been said. I told someone afterwards that more people came by to shake hands with me then with Kay Bailey Hutchinson."

In late July 2008, Jack received notice that the Experienced Workers Organization had selected him as the Outstanding Older Worker in the state of Texas for 2008. This designation is awarded by the U.S. Department of Labor. The objective is to encourage older people who desired employment to seek courses and education necessary to qualify them for gainful employment of their choosing.

Each year 53 recipients are selected from the contiguous states, Washington D.C and Puerto Rico. A meeting was held in Washington D.C. honoring one outstanding older person from each state or district. A special designation went to the oldest person receiving one of the recognitions. Jack missed being the oldest by four months. A woman from Nebraska who was just four months older than Jack bested him. During the weeklong activities, Jack visited 2 senators from Texas. He said that Kay Granger was no doubt the most memorable. Kay Granger presented Jack a box during the visit.

When he opened the box it contained a U.S. Flag and a certificate that stated, "This Flag of the United States of America was flown over the United States Capitol, at the request of Honorable Kay Granger and members of Congress. In honor of Texas' 2008 Outstanding Older Worker of the Year, Mr. Jack Borden and his extraordinary history of service to his community, his clients, his county and his country."

Jack stated that this was a real fine meeting and that he enjoyed the entire trip and was delighted with the work of the U.S. Dept of Labor in presenting these awards.

Jack was honored in the Nov 2008 Texas Bar Journal, Vol.71, No.10, as a "Living Legend." The full-page article was complemented with a color picture of Jack Borden and highlighted all of his 100 years of life up to date, 2008.

During an interview in Nov. 2008 Jack stated that almost everyone likes to see his or her name in print or photograph in, a magazine or newspaper. He expressed his thanks to the Parker County Today Magazine, the Weatherford Star Telegram and Weatherford Democrat for the articles about him, his life and achievements. He expressed a special thanks to Mary Kemp, Leon Tanner, Jamie Bodiford-Brinkly and the people in his office for all the good things they have done for him. Jack said a very special thank you to Rose Paige, his caretaker, for personally submitting his name for the Experienced Worker award. In retrospect Jack stated, "Of all the good things that have happened to me there have been some sad things. I lost my wife of 66 years, on October 22, 2006. I give her credit for a great deal of the good things that have happened to me."

Parker County and Weatherford citizens are indeed proud of Jack and Edith Borden. Thanks Jack for your unwavering dedication and support for community, state and country.